OTTO WOOD,
THE BANDIT

OTTO WOOD,
THE BANDIT

THE FREIGHTHOPPING THIEF, BOOTLEGGER, AND CONVICTED MURDERER ☞ BEHIND THE ☜ APPALACHIAN BALLADS

Trevor McKenzie

FOREWORD BY DAVID HOLT

THE UNIVERSITY OF NORTH CAROLINA PRESS
CHAPEL HILL

Published with the assistance of
the H. Eugene and Lillian Lehman Fund
of the University of North Carolina Press.

Designed by April Leidig
Set in Arnhem by Copperline Book Services, Inc.
Manufactured in the United States of America

The University of North Carolina Press has been a
member of the Green Press Initiative since 2003.

Cover illustration from the author's collection

Library of Congress Cataloging-in-Publication Data
Names: McKenzie, Trevor, author. |
Holt, David, 1946– writer of foreword.
Title: Otto Wood, the bandit : the freighthopping thief,
bootlegger, and convicted murderer behind the Appalachian
ballads / Trevor McKenzie ; foreword by David Holt.
Description: Chapel Hill : The University of North Carolina
Press, 2021. | Includes bibliographical references and index.
Identifiers: LCCN 2021019308 | ISBN 9781469665665 (cloth) |
ISBN 9781469664712 (pbk ; alk. paper) | ISBN 9781469664729 (ebook)
Subjects: LCSH: Wood, Otto, 1895–1930. | Criminals—North Carolina—
Biography. | Criminals—Appalachian Region, Southern—Biography. |
Appalachian Region, Southern—Folklore. | LCGFT: Biographies.
Classification: LCC HV6248.W725 M35 2021 | DDC 364.152/3092 [B]—dc23
LC record available at https://lccn.loc.gov/2021019308

FOR HERB

"OTTO, WHY DIDN'T YOU RUN?"

⚡⚡⚡

CONTENTS

FIGURES

FOREWORD

AFTER OTTO WOOD DIED in a hail of gunfire in Salisbury, North Carolina, six thousand people came to view his body. That was more than one-third of the population of the town in 1930. Otto had captivated the public imagination with his bravado, relentless law-breaking, and good humor. His eleven daring escapes from five penitentiaries captured the imagination of the press and the public. North Carolinians waited for the next chapter of his exploits. And he did all this with a clubfoot and a missing hand.

Otto Wood wasn't a particularly violent man. Most of his crimes were for running moonshine and stealing cars (and anything else not tied down). At seven years old he stole a bicycle. The sheriff caught Otto pushing the bike down the road because the youngster didn't know how to ride it. At ten years old he ran away to West Virginia to stay with his Hatfield cousins. There he learned how to fight from infamous Hatfields and became proficient at gambling, making whiskey, and driving fast. Running moonshine was as natural to him as it was to many other people in Wilkes County, North Carolina, in the days of Prohibition. White liquor was the best way to turn corn into cash.

The song "Otto Wood the Bandit," written and released shortly after Otto's death, has kept his name and his legacy before the public. Walter Kid Smith wrote it in 1931 and recorded it with his group the Carolina Buddies. The recording sold 2,713 copies, a respectable number considering it was in the middle of the Depression. Thirty-four years later, Doc Watson, the legendary blind guitarist and singer from western North Carolina, recorded the song on his 1965 album *Doc Watson and Son*. This was in the burgeoning days of the folk music revival. As interest in folk music grew, other musicians influenced by Watson added the song to their repertoires. Today the song remains one of the enduring ballads of mountain music.

Once, while on tour with Doc, I asked him where he learned "Otto Wood the Bandit." He said his father worked in a sawmill for a week in trade for a windup Victrola and fifty 78 rpm records. Because the cost of a record could equal a man's daily wage, Doc's father supplemented the young guitarist's record collection by growing bushes and fruit trees to trade with his neighbors to get new records for his son. "Otto Wood the Bandit" came in trade for a little boxwood.

Doc Watson grew up near the border of Wilkes County, North Carolina, so it was only natural that the Watson family would have heard gossip and stories about Otto. Watson told me the locals thought of Wood as something of a Robin Hood. But as Doc reiterated, "Otto didn't give a whole lot to the poor."

Doc told a very detailed version of how Otto Wood came to kill Mr. Kaplan the pawnbroker, and told another tale about how Otto carved a fake gun out of a bar of soap when in prison. Doc said Otto used the soap gun to surprise a guard and make an escape. This is in all likelihood pure folklore. John Dillinger did make a gun out of wood to escape, but there is no record of Otto Wood using the same trick. It was a folktale in the making.

During one of his stints in the state prison in Raleigh, Wood penned his autobiography and sold each copy for fifty cents. The slim volume clearly shows that Wood was an excellent raconteur when telling his rambunctious life story. In 1984 I interviewed Jesse James Bailey, the sheriff of both Madison and Buncombe Counties in western North Carolina during Prohibition. He told me about the time he arrested Otto Wood in Buncombe County and personally drove him to the maximum-security penitentiary in Raleigh. Bailey said Wood regaled them with jokes and stories all the way to the prison and kept Jesse and his deputy thoroughly entertained for the eight-hour drive. Bailey recalled that when they got to the Raleigh prison, everyone greeted Otto with open arms and shouts of "Did you bring any liquor with you?"

In 1999 I was doing a concert in Charlotte, North Carolina, and played my banjo version of the song "Otto Wood." After the show Linda Luther came backstage and introduced herself as Otto Wood's granddaughter. Her mother was Pearl and her grandmother was Otto's wife, Rushey. I was thrilled and astounded to actually meet his descendants. Linda and I have stayed in touch since that time. She said her mother rarely mentioned Otto Wood when Linda was a child for fear friends and neighbors would look down on them. Linda and her sisters followed some of the stories they had heard about their grandfather. They visited Otto Wood's grave in Coaldale, West Virginia. One of the local historians told them that because of the big turnout to view Otto's corpse in Salisbury, the family was concerned that someone would steal the body and put it on display. The family laid sticks in a subtle pattern on the grave so they could tell if grave robbers tried to steal the body. But Otto was able to rest in peace.

But his compelling story and the jaunty ballad keep bringing people back to explore the life of this one-armed bandit. Now we have this carefully researched and deeply thoughtful account of Wood's life. Thanks to Trevor McKenzie, we now know more about Otto Wood and the world he lived in than we've ever known before. If you enjoy true crime, southern history, or traditional music, *Otto Wood, the Bandit* is a book you don't want to miss.

David Holt
Asheville, NC

OTTO WOOD,
THE BANDIT

INTRODUCTION

THE SILHOUETTES of two men in overcoats emerge into the light, their feet scraping on gravel. Their conversation is muffled as one limps his way closer to an unseen audience, obscured in the darkness, nonexistent aside from the creak of a metal chair and an occasional cough. Two more silhouettes emerge, one in a broad-brimmed hat. The voices get louder, followed by several wild glints, flashes of pistols pulled hastily from pockets, then sharp metallic clicks and the rapid explosion of gunfire. The shadow of the limping man staggers a few more paces and falls to the ground.

For the audience, these characters are spotlighted, every line heard and gesture seen before the shots ring out. From where I am seated, though, all is shadow; the action is just out of sight, hidden by a wall on the side of the stage. I may not be able to see anything, but the gunfire tells me all I need to know: Otto Wood is dead, again.

It is July 2014 in North Wilkesboro, North Carolina, the fourth year of the outdoor drama *Otto Wood: The Bandit*. This play is how a community reenacts and remembers the life and times of their infamous, homegrown bandit. For the audience, the scene is the cold midday of New Year's Eve 1930, but back in the darkness on the side stage with the other musicians of the Elkville String Band, it is sweltering. It sounds like the cicadas from the woods behind us might just have the last song in tonight's performance. The dramatic tension playing out upstage is not my worry, but the tension of my fiddle bow is. The hair will not budge, the workings of the frog jammed by the humidity. The legs of my overalls stick to the edge of the metal chair. I look down to see a woolly aphid, a parasite fallen from a tree in the back of park latched onto the snakewood stick of my bow. I flick the small cotton-like freeloader off into the darkness.

It's almost time to play. The lights go down, then flick back on. That's our cue. In the chair next to me, seated with a brown fedora tilted slightly down over his eyes, guitarist Herb Key begins to sing the words he's sung a thousand times, the opening lines of the ballad "Otto Wood the Bandit":

Step up, buddies, and listen to my song,
I'll sing it to you right but you might sing it wrong,
Story 'bout a man they called Otto Wood . . .

The story of Otto Wood is as twisty as the lyrics of the ballad that bears his name. Composed in 1931 by Walter "Kid" Smith and originally performed by Smith's group, the Carolina Buddies, the song is now known in folk music circles worldwide—thanks in no small part to a 1960s recording by noted North Carolina guitarist and singer Arthel "Doc" Watson. Smith's composition is just one of many Otto Wood ballads, however, and, like all outlaw ballads, it selectively distills the complicated life story of a real criminal. The combination of a bouncy melody with violent lyrics is strikingly dissonant. With a chorus pleading "Otto, why didn't you run?," the song begs for more facts. This is a true crime story hidden behind a ballad.

Otto Wood's life was full of running, a surprising amount of running for someone born with a clubbed left foot. With beginnings in rural Wilkes County, North Carolina, at the end of the nineteenth century, Wood's life of crime started in his preteen years and extended for three decades. By the time he entered his early teens, Wood was sentenced to work on a chain gang. Only a few years later, he was one of the first children from the mountains of western North Carolina sent to a new state reformatory. By the age of eighteen, he had racked up a list of petty thefts, as well as escapes from chain gangs and the reformatory, and he had lost his left hand in a hunting accident.

Despite the misfortunes of his early years, Wood packed a lot of adventure into his short life. Wood's criminal activities led him through the deserts of south Texas, the railyards of Missouri and West Virginia, and the back roads of North Carolina. His prison record reflects his travels, as well as his savvy as an escape artist. Within the span of seventeen years, between 1913 and 1930, Wood escaped eleven times from five different state penitentiaries across the South and Midwest. These escapes are in addition to breaks from smaller jails, too numerous and, at times, too obscured in the records to ever be tallied. Wood, like many criminals of the era, also loved a good alias and used many throughout his life, further hindering any effort to trace his criminal activities.

In the mid-1920s, Wood achieved a semicelebrity status throughout the southern United States as the "Houdini of Cell Block A," a prisoner no jail or penitentiary could hold. His notoriety and crimes caught the attention of several North Carolina governors, most notably O. Max Gardner, who met with Wood and attempted to use the escape artist as a poster child for prison reform. The result of what Gardner termed an "Experiment in Humanity" proved disastrous and ultimately led to the manhunt that resulted in Wood's death at the age of thirty-seven. A shootout on the streets of Salisbury on New Year's Eve 1930 ended Wood's life, but inspired lyrical tributes from early country music songsters who gave Wood a path, albeit a belated one, to immortality.

Can't tell you all but I wish I could . . .

Even the ballad lyrics reveal the difficulties of documenting Otto Wood's life. True to his larger-than-life persona, Wood took the liberty of writing his autobiography, titled *Life History of Otto Wood*, while behind the walls of the North Carolina State Prison in 1926. While the book contains some solid stretches of narrative on Wood's life, the numerous half-truths and embellishments padded around the facts make the work well short of anything that could be considered a true history. For example, in one passage, Wood and "his girl"—there is always a female companion in Wood's stories—travel through the Colorado River area of Arizona, where they are surrounded one night by a "hundred or more angry wolves." A few pages later, a Texas lawman tells Wood to "reach for the clouds." Wood obliges, telling his readers that he remembered "the Western rule not to shoot a man so long as his hands were in the air." If these passages sound like dime novel scenes or straight of an early 1900s Saturday cowboy serial, it's because they likely are. Wood, while he did commit real crimes in the American Southwest, consumed and indulged in cowboy and Old West outlaw stories. Descriptions of his crimes in newspapers bear out that Wood frequently and consciously playacted the role of the man with—to quote country music legend Marty Robbins—a "big iron on his hip." As further evidence, a 1913 photo sent to his mother from Texas shows Wood leveling an antiquated Colt pistol at the camera, wearing the ten-gallon hat and fur chaps of a typical silver screen desperado.

Even with this intermittent Tom Mix–style bravado, Wood could not obscure the fact he was a product of a modernizing Appalachian South. He was a car thief, a bootlegger, a train robber, and an escape artist who had all the latest technologies available at the fingertips of his remaining hand. He also made sure to place his one good foot into the criminal networks around illegal alcohol and the trafficking of stolen cars. Although Wood had all the hallmarks of a criminal genius—his miraculous escapes, even when undertaken with accomplices, were mostly accomplished through his own ingenuity—his long stints of avoiding the law were aided by a highly organized community surrounding the production and distribution of illegal liquor. This connection to "moonshine" made his home community in Wilkes County the epicenter for Wood's crimes. The people in the criminal networks surrounding illegal liquor, as production ramped up under the conditions of Prohibition, needed Wood's talents as a driver and were ultimately Wood's safety net. Nevertheless, Wood's *Life History* is how he wanted his story told, and this version of his life must be given some respect and consideration. Truth was, no doubt in Wood's mind, just another cell with a lock to pick.

This work is intended to provide compelling biography of a criminal who emerged from the modernizing Appalachian South of the early twentieth century. Through a combination of prison records, newspapers accounts, oral histories, and myriad other sources, I have constructed, to the best of my ability, a narrative history of the life and crimes of Otto Wood. At certain points, I defer to Wood's own account and words in his *Life History*. These points of deferral, however, often juxtapose Wood's stories with prison records or newspaper reports. Throughout the book, narrative gaps of several months appear as Wood travels the highways and back roads from point A to point B, or languishes behind prison bars. I hope readers will excuse these gaps, as I have focused on the events and velocity of a fast-paced narrative suitable to the life Otto Wood lived. Countless family stories and many small facets of Wood's life are no doubt absent. I look forward to hearing more stories about Otto Wood, and I see this work as a starting point for a renewed conversation about Wood's significance as a criminal and as a folk hero. When it comes to Otto Wood, just as the ballad reminds us, I "can't tell you all, but I wish could."

CHAPTER 1

TIME AMONG STRANGERS

CHILDHOOD AND EARLY CRIMES,

1893–1912

Wood was born and raised in the Ronda section of Wilkes county, in country traversed by what is now the Boone trail. His people are said to have been good, law abiding people, but he turned out to be the black sheep of the family.
—*Mount Airy (NC) News*, December 3, 1925

Harrison is a small boy. . . . He says his father is dead and that his mother and several brothers and sisters are living in Wilkes and that it was hard to be taken from them and brought to a strange county to serve his time among strangers and be treated as a criminal.
—*Charlotte (NC) Observer*, August 27, 1907

Otto Wood, we are told, was mighty brave and bold,
Who once was a brakeman on a train,
But in a wreck one day,
He lost his hand they say . . .
—"Otto Wood," recorded by Cranford and Thompson,
    Champion 17486, January 27, 1931, Richmond, Indiana

I N THE FALL OF 1985, the *Wilkes (NC) Journal-Patriot* decided to memorialize one of Wilkes County's most infamous sons. Prying into the memories of elder residents located throughout the county, the small-town newshawks sought out locals' recollections of Otto Harrison Wood. The outlaw's roots in the county had, in the half century since his final shootout, grown into a tangle of mesmeric stories full of adventure and rife with inconsistencies. Relayed both first- and secondhand, the anecdotes surrounding Wood's earliest years illumined childhood scenes with perspectives altogether distinct from those previously recorded in the outlaw's own account of his life. Featured prominently was a brief reminiscence from Fannie Buchanan, the midwife who had delivered the child that grew up to become a bandit. The chief thought in Fannie's mind was the tough delivery caused by Wood's feet, which she had later placed in splints "to prevent them from turning inward." Despite Fannie's work, Otto's left foot remained clubbed in adulthood, a characteristic used by lawmen to profile Wood in his repeated flights from the prison cell. "Mrs. Buchanan said in later years," quipped one of Wood's relatives, "that if she had known he was going to spend his life running from the law, she wouldn't have fixed his feet." Buchanan's lighthearted regret sprang from the benefit of hindsight, a knowledge that the child she helped bring into the world left a legacy of criminal exploits that extended across the nation during his lifetime.[1]

The area where Otto Wood spent his early childhood was a farming community known as Dellaplane in the northeastern section of Wilkes County. Shadowed by the low, rounded peaks of the Brushy Mountains, the world that greeted this child presented an atmosphere not altogether hospitable to those with any kind of handicap, a world dependent on the physical strength of families for day-to-day labor. Termed "hoe farmers" by their eastern counterparts, the rural residents of these foothills and mountain areas lived on the far periphery of the cash crops market that dominated the lowland South, and they worked comparatively small tracts of land.[2] Though markedly diminutive in size, these acreages situated along the eastern slope of the Blue Ridge featured a prime landscape for farming families engaged in a broad spectrum of vocations. Where the valleys held a high fertile potential for crops such as wheat and corn, the hillocks interspersed between the Brushys and the Blue Ridge sheltered the pasturing of livestock as well as the growth of productive apple orchards.[3]

Despite the beauty and bounty provided by the land, the reality of farm life in the foothills of North Carolina presented an image, as one chronicler termed it, "far removed from an agrarian paradise of yeomen."[4] Although the Wood family owned their home and land, they suffered like other western North Carolinians under a tax system that considered the potential productivity of their acreage. As historian Dwight Billings explains, an "antiquated tax structure placed an unequal burden on agrarians at a time when corporate taxes were minimized to encourage industrial development."[5] Only six years after Wood's birth, the 1900 census noted that 26,872 people resided within Wilkes County, and most of them inhabited the roughly 2,565 farms within the region.[6] The separation of this region from the wider agrarian interests of other North Carolinians in the decades immediately after the Civil War proved at least moderately beneficial. These hill-and-valley farmers long used to engaging in a wide variety of pursuits then enjoyed some prosperity, while their neighbors in the Piedmont and East starved and suffered under the near feudal conditions of tenant farming, a way of life that catered to industrial cotton and tobacco.

Named for English parliamentarian John Wilkes, Wood's home county had played host to a number of singular characters throughout its history. Formed from a section of neighboring Surry County in 1777, it was an area once explored by Moravians, who visited from their established settlements a hundred miles to the south in the mid-1700s. The expedition of these Central European settlers stopped short of a Cherokee village located on the north bank of the Yadkin River. According to local lore, the Moravians left the area after discovering that the consistency of the Yadkin's clay made it unsuitable for their style of pottery.[7] During the Revolutionary War, noted Tory-hunter Colonel Benjamin Cleveland used the region as a base to further the patriot cause, his progress evidenced by the number of tree limbs reportedly bearing the hanging corpses of Loyalists.[8] Two prominent later settlers, Chang and Eng Bunker, the original "Siamese Twins," moved (and married) into the county in the mid-nineteenth century; the duo sought a place for retirement after a decade of touring. Only a few decades later, the personal affairs of a Wilkes native, Confederate veteran Thomas C. Dula, had threatened to reignite the politics of the Civil War in a now infamous Statesville murder trial.

The Wood family shared in the history of Wilkes County for over a century prior to Otto's birth. Otto's great-grandfather Thomas Wood was born in the county around the year 1785.[9] Thomas's parents, Joseph Wood and Catharine Day—natives of Virginia and Pennsylvania, respectively— entered the county at unknown date during the mid-1700s. In the early spring of 1808, Thomas married Margaret "Peggy" Durham of neighboring Iredell County; his father, Joseph, acted as bondsman.[10] Peggy later claimed a pension for Thomas's service within the ranks of Captain Carlton's company of the North Carolina militia during the War of 1812.[11] Thomas's son Reuben, born in 1827, farmed a section of the Rock Creek community and married Ellender "Nellie" Johnson. Their second-youngest child, Otto's father, Thomas H. Wood, was born sometime between 1861 and 1863.[12] Thomas married Amelia Ellen Staley, Otto's mother, at the home of her father, Joseph Staley, in December 1882.[13] The Staleys were also a deep-seated Wilkes County family with roots in the county stretching back to the early nineteenth century.

By the time of Otto Wood's birth on May 9, 1893, the courtship of the predominantly agrarian region of Wilkes County with industrial development progressed rapidly with the construction of a rail line north from Winston. Completed in 1891, this spur of the Norfolk and Southern line terminated just across the Yadkin River from the county seat of Wilkesboro. The new community surrounding the railhead, dubbed North Wilkesboro, gradually expanded as the county's center for industry and commerce. This rail hub initially serviced the timber industry, but by the 1910s the area also held mills engaged in the processing of corn and cotton. Tanneries and furniture factories followed the mills as the town's population swelled. North Wilkesboro became the gateway to the "lost provinces" of the western North Carolina mountains, a place where the raw materials of agriculture and the timber industry were collected, processed, and shipped to far areas of the lowland South. A report from the North Carolina Department of Agriculture boasted of the railroad's effect on the region, opening up "a section heretofore accessible only with difficulty."[14]

Otto spent his earliest years in the vicinity of North Wilkesboro and probably witnessed the beginnings of the area's industrial growth during his childhood. In 1900, the town reported a population of 918 people, many of whom still listed their occupation as either farmworker or day laborer. Listed as both "Emelia" and "Ellen Wood" in the 1900 census, Wood's mother gave her first recorded occupation as dressmaker. Thomas Wood had succumbed to typhoid fever sometime around 1898, leaving Ellen as the only provider for the family. At thirty-five years old, Amelia Ellen Staley Wood was a widow who claimed to have borne seven children, four of whom survived: James, age sixteen; Luther, twelve; Otto (ironically enough, spelled "Auto" on the census), six; and Robert, four.[15]

In 1910, the family reported their home at Antioch, a small farming community located in the east-central portion of Wilkes County. Ellen Wood provided her occupation as farmer with sons Otto H., reported as fifteen (a year or so off from the commonly recorded birthday May 1893), and Robert L., thirteen, listed as farm laborers. In a situation akin to that of other small farming families, the Wood household may not have been wealthy, but the family did own their farm outright, free of mortgages. Two more children—daughters Irene, age eight, and Ellen M., six—are also listed as part of the Wood family. Otto explained these additions to the family in an interview for the report *Capital Punishment in North Carolina*, published in 1929:

> [Otto's] father and mother, who were in fairly good circumstances, lived on a farm where he lived until he was eight years old. He states that his father died when was very young, and about a year afterwards

his mother "took up" with a married man, by whom she had two il-
legitimate children. He claims that he and the younger children were
neglected and allowed to run wild and do what they chose. Still, he has
always had love for his mother, and since she has grown older, he has
protected her and provided for her when he could. He says he feels no
resentment toward her.[16]

Although this offers some explanation for two additional daughters in the
Wood household, Otto's narrative as recounted by the examiner in *Capital
Punishment* must be looked at with a scrutinizing eye. Wood was not above
embellishing his life's story, yet it does seem unlikely he would purposefully
construct a narrative that placed any negative light on his mother, his most
consistent ally throughout his life. Perhaps corroborating Wood's story, a
listing of cases seen before the superior court in Wilkes County dated August 8, 1902, lists Ellen Wood as appearing before the court on charges of
"fornication and adultery."[17] The *North Wilkesboro Hustler* notes that the
prosecutor dropped the case against Ellen before it went to trial.

Ellen sent Otto to school at age seven but, as Wood himself later acknowledged, he showed a marked lack of affinity for education. To be sure, there
was little to recommend the formal instruction he chose not to receive.
As in many other rural areas of the South, the school system in Wilkes
County suffered due to its ineffectual structure that entailed "too many
school districts, poor housing facilities . . . poorly prepared teachers . . .
[and] poorly compensated teachers."[18] In his *Life History*, Wood recalled his
classmates chiding him for his raggedy clothes as the main cause for his
"playing hookey." Wood apparently attended school just enough to make an
impression on one of these instructors, Mrs. Mattie Sale. As recorded in *Lest
We Forget: Education in Wilkes, 1778–1978*, Mrs. Sale "lived to see many of
her students become successful teachers, preachers, dentists, lawyers, and
prosperous farmers in her native county. Her one regret was Otto Wood, a
noted outlaw. . . . She remembered him as a normal and obedient boy who
became a notorious outlaw."[19] Wood was not as kind to other instructors,
later recalling that he struck a teacher with a slate after the man meted out
punishment on his younger brother, Robert.[20] Perhaps the one small victory
in Otto's formal education, listed in the 1910 census, was his ability at age
fifteen to read and write.[21]

Aside from those newspaper stories describing Wood's criminal activities and the information offered by Wood in his *Life History*, there are a
slim number of accounts that shed light on Otto's childhood personality.
By Wood's own recollection, he spent most of his boyhood in the mountains

surrounding North Wilkesboro. In the North Carolina State Prison's report *Capital Punishment in North Carolina*, Wood expressed to his interviewer an early interest in music, hunting, and exploring in the Brushy Mountains. He reported playing music on the fiddle and banjo, learning by ear, without formal musical training. Local lore reports that after he lost his left hand, he strapped a spoon to his wrist to play the banjo like a slide guitar—similar to a style picked by fellow Wilkes Countian Dock Walsh.[22] "At the age of five I would slip away into the woods and spend the day trying to find things in hollow trees and rock cliffs," Wood recalled in his *Life History* (1926). As with many other children in the rural areas of the North Carolina mountains, the newly built railroad lines caused him to dream of travel: "I appeared to crave adventure and the sound of a locomotive whistle seemed to put new life into me as I considered it a call to go somewhere."[23] A 1916 article in the *Charlotte Observer* remarked on this early wanderlust and detailed Wood's local reputation as a child hobo. Slipping behind a coal tender of a passenger train, Wood had apparently once hoboed to Winston-Salem and then, soon thereafter, to the 1904 St. Louis Exposition, from which he came back with a (presumably stolen) profit of twenty cents.[24]

As a sickly child with a clubfoot, Wood escaped punishment for many of his earliest crimes through pity and the protection of his mother. W. P. Byrd, whom the press dubbed Otto Wood's "father-in-law by adoption" in 1931, later recalled in an interview: "'I've been a-knowing Otto since he was a little boy . . . just so high' and he indicated with his hand distance of about two feet from the floor. 'The first thing I remember him doing was stealing guns from hardware stores in Wilkes County and selling them. And I guess he has been stealing ever since.'"[25] The article that held Byrd's interview described how "Ellen Wood used to go around . . . gathering up all these guns . . . taking them back to the stores and begging off for her boy."[26] In one such episode, Wood sold three guns to a wagoner who, on paying the boy, turned his back, only to have Otto steal the weapons to sell again. Wood then "took [the guns] out in the country and sold them to an old woman" from whom he promptly stole them a third time.[27] Byrd qualified his comments on Wood's childhood demeanor by acknowledging a consensus among Wilkes residents that, although a criminal, Wood seemed especially "generous," sharing the profits from his crimes with friends and family.[28]

In an oral history collected for the Old Wilkes Jail Museum, Ruth Wood Holbrook said Otto's generous nature was one of the factors that drove him to life of crime:

Otto Wood was my grandfather's uncle. . . . His first robbing, I have been told, was on his birthday, I think somewhere around 6 or while he was still a boy and his mother worked for a family in Wilkesboro and she told them that she would take her pay in fatback meat, instead of the 50 cent she usually got, and that it was his (Otto's) birthday and that he wanted fatback meat, cream gravy, eggs, and biscuits for his supper. She worked from 6 that morning till 6 that night and they told her they would get they would get the meat for their dinner and they went to the smoke house and got a bunch, whole bag full of old rancid meat skins that had skippers on them and they told her that was a pay. . . . When she got home she did not have no meat but she made his supper out of lard. . . . He (Otto) left and went and robbed the store that belonged to the people where she worked that day. He robbed the store that night and he left. He took the food. He got food and feed for the horse or mule, whichever it was, and he left home.[29]

Mrs. Holbrook's memory of Otto Wood, though handed down from family lore, has several hallmarks not entirely in line with the few known facts about Wood's history. Aside from this anecdote about Wood's earliest crime, Mrs. Holbrook asserted that Wood's father died in a railroad accident instead of typhoid fever. Adding yet another shadow of doubt, the gun that Mrs. Holbrook donated to the museum along with this oral history proved to have a date of manufacture well after Otto's death in the 1930. Despite these inconsistencies, the tale constitutes an interesting addition to the lore surrounding Wood's early years.

The first criminal activity reported in the press concerning Otto Wood appeared in the *Wilkesboro Chronicle* in December 1904. "Otto Woods [sic], a youngster about nine years old, is in jail for breaking into McGee's store last week and carrying out a lot of guns," the *Hustler* reported. Wood was described as having already stolen a bicycle, which placed him in front of the court earlier in the fall.[30] Wood remembered the bicycle theft in his *Life History*, recalling that his inability to ride it attracted the attention of a local policeman.[31] Put on trial in January 1905, Wilkes County justice of the peace G. W. Upchurch sent Wood and his accomplice, William Caudill, another local boy, to serve jail time for larceny.[32] Upchurch again sentenced Wood to jail time in April 1907, for stealing a boat and floating it down the Yadkin River. Wood and his companions, John Robinson and Tom Moore, sold the stolen vessel somewhere farther downstream. By the time of their capture, the youthful gang hid or spent enough of the money from the boat to render themselves unable to pay the fines imposed by the court—not that the court would have accepted the money anyway.[33]

The string of petty thefts culminated in August 1907, when Wood, now a teenager, was sentenced to the Iredell County chain gang for carrying a concealed weapon. An article in the *Statesville Landmark* gave a surprising amount of detail on the young prisoner:

> It was mentioned in the last issue of *The Landmark* that Otto Wood of Wilkes county was now a recruit for the Iredell chain gang. Wood is a small white boy about 14 years old and was sentenced to the gang by Judge Ward at the last term of the Wilkes court for carrying a concealed weapon. He was brought to Statesville Saturday by Sheriff Brown of Wilkes and has begun his four month term. *The Landmark* reporter visited Wood and found him to be a bright and intelligent young fellow. He is somewhat of a cripple—one leg being smaller than the other— but is active and says he attended school part of his time and worked in the stores of his brothers, Messrs. J. A. and L. T. Wood, at and near North Wilkesboro. His father is dead but his mother and several broth- ers and sisters reside at North Wilkesboro. He told a pathetic story of how his people tried to get the judge to change the sentence to a lite [*sic*] and of the parting at home when he had to leave his family and be brought here among strangers. He of course claims that the pistol he had was nothing but a toy and that enemies swore that they had seen him with a real pistol.
>
> The case caused much sympathy for the boy at the court house and jail Saturday and Sherriff Brown asked that he be allowed privileges at the gang camp. It is a pity there is not a reformatory or training school for youths of this age type. To put them on a chain gang where they are thrown with criminals of all classes means that they will most prob- ably lose all self-respect and will become hardened. The fact that a boy has been on the chain gang will also be against him all his life.[34]

Wood's own memories of the event, constructed much later, conflicted with those given to Statesville reporters. By Otto's recollection, his older broth- ers, who, according to *The Landmark*, employed him in their stores, were unduly cruel to him.[35] In Wood's account, one of these elder siblings, when asked by a judge to take Otto under his wing, responded that "he had tried and failed" and "could not do anything."[36] The truth concerning his neglect at the hands of his older brothers more than likely sits somewhere between these two narratives.

The sentencing of a teenager to the Iredell County chain gang incited a dialogue in regional newspapers concerning Wood's age and intelligence as well as the need for the state of North Carolina to establish an alternative punishment for children who committed criminal acts. A reporter for the *Charlotte Observer* profiled Wood—going by his middle name, "Harrison"— during his stay in the prison at Statesville. After meeting with Wood, the *Observer* correspondent remarked on the teenager's proclivity for reading, noting, "He also asked for good literature to read during spare time at the chain gang."[37] Seeing Wood's case as an embodiment of a greater societal problem, the reporter posited that North Carolina was severely in need of a reformatory. The *North Wilkesboro Hustler* countered the *Observer*'s sympathetic angle on Wood's case: "The youth and disability of the boy is pathetic and it is a pity that the State has not provided for him, but at the same time North Wilkesboro is glad to get rid of the boy. He is generally known here as a menacing rogue and has become a local by-word, and [is] dreaded by the community."[38] The North Wilkesboro writer's sentiments would be echoed in the coming decades during Wood's frequent returns home after criminal activities extending across the nation.

Almost in response to the report from Wilkesboro, Wood attempted to escape from the Iredell chain gang camp on the morning of September 8, 1907, boarding a train at the nearby community of Eufola. Aware of his escape and penchant for train-hopping, officers waited at the Statesville station and captured Wood as he disembarked that evening.[39] A month later, Iredell county officials moved Wood from the chain gang to jail after he displayed signs of "chills and malarial fever."[40] Wood returned home in October 1907, his release attributed to concerns for his health and his inability to work on the chain gang due to the deformity of his left leg.[41] Concerns for Wood's health and his physical state would continue to elicit the sympathy of prison officials throughout his life. Wardens would often assign Wood to menial jobs, such as a water boy for the chain gang, unwittingly placing him in the perfect position to effect an escape.

In April 1908 Wood's proclivity for taking other children's bicycles once again landed him in trouble. In addition to stealing the bicycle of another local boy, Charles Fletcher, Wood broke into the E. L. Hart Company hardware store in North Wilkesboro. The young bandit then absconded south toward Taylorsville with "six pocket, pearl handle knives, and one Smith and Wesson pistol." Using the relatively new technology of telephone, authorities in Wilkes County quickly alerted their counterparts in neighboring counties to keep a lookout for Wood. Police in Taylorsville captured Wood and held him until Officer D. S. Lane arrived from Wilkes to retrieve him. In the first of many fights over Wood's custody, Lane and Taylorsville officers clashed over the issue of jail fees and meals served to Wood during his stay. Meeting in the street, Lane argued with the town's mayor and the jailer, refusing to pay the "three or four dollars" of jail fees. Unable to reach an agreement, Lane headed back to North Wilkesboro, but only made a few miles of the journey before he was flagged down and handed a telephone message telling him to halt. Moments later, a Taylorsville officer arrived by double-team buggy with Wood and the stolen bicycle in the seat beside him. Before the exchange could commence, Wood leaped from the buggy and ran into a nearby pine thicket. The Taylorsville officer pursued him a short distance before recapturing him and handing him back over to Lane. The officers discovered a sum of around seven dollars hidden in Wood's stocking, but he refused to tell them where the money had come from.[42]

The punishment Wood received for this crime spree appears not to have reached the severity of the chain gang sentence from a year earlier. No doubt the portrait of the child-turned-criminal as a "pathetic case," featured in regional newspapers the previous fall, assured that Wood received a relatively lenient jail sentence. Officials likely knew that sending Wood back to the chain gang would only reignite public commentary on the ethics of sending a partially crippled teenager to work alongside grown men sentenced to hard labor for more serious crimes.[43]

In February 1909, Wood's theft of chewing gum and change from a slot machine in Winston, North Carolina, once again landed him in trouble with the law.[44] Instead of returning him to the chain gang, the court in Winston decided to send Wood to the newly created Stonewall Jackson Training School in Concord, North Carolina.[45] Wood lied to officials, saying that he was only thirteen years old, roughly the same age as when he was sentenced to the chain gang two years earlier, and claimed he had worked for a lumber company in High Point prior to becoming stranded in Winston. Members of the court, well aware of Wood's time on the Iredell chain gang, expressed less sympathy and more skepticism than they had in previous cases against Wood. A clerk noted that Wood had been seen "hanging around the depot here for sometime past," and police deliberately questioned the age of the young prisoner, remarking that he seemed "more than 13 years of age."[46] At this early age, Wood was already manipulating his image to try to sway the public and the law in his favor. Although this attempt failed, he would become more expert in this type of manipulation over the coming decades.

Established in 1907, largely in response to the well-publicized backlash against such cases as Wood's chain gang sentence, the Stonewall Jackson Training School provided an alternative to jail time for young white males between the ages of twelve and sixteen. The foundation of this reform school was part of a larger "uplift movement" among southern elites, one that ultimately intended to educate and make better citizens and voters—preferably non-Republican and nonpopulist voters—out of rural southern whites.[47] A column in the *Union Republican* of Winston-Salem focused on Wood's significance as "Forsyth's first contribution to this establishment which recently began business for the moral uplift of young law-breakers."[48] The main structure of the Training School was a hulking, white-columned structure. Like many other reform schools of the era, the institution was not without its share of physical and psychological abuses that harmed its pupils more than helped them. Almost confirming himself as a victim of these, Wood never mentioned his time in the Stonewall Jackson Training School in his *Life History* or in his interview for *Capital Punishment*, choosing instead to focus on visits to his family in West Virginia.

From the beginning, Wood's childhood, centered in the hills of Wilkes County, yielded a "pan-Appalachian" experience. The rail lines along the base of North Carolina's Blue Ridge ran through the mountains of Virginia and from there west to the coalfields of West Virginia and eastern Kentucky. For Wood and other young men in the counties of western North Carolina, the new railroads provided a "means of escape, their ticket to adventure, a new life of opportunity, and excitement."[49] Wood remembered that from his earliest years he had heard stories of an uncle "engaged in the saloon business on [the] Tug River, Mingo County," which was located in the heart of the coalfields along the Kentucky border.[50] The 1900 census lists Wood's uncle, Joseph Staley, as a "day laborer" working in Mingo County.[51]

During Wood's childhood, the saloons in the coal towns along the Tug River possessed a reputation that rivaled the fictionalized portrayals of the Wild West. According to one recent examination, the proliferation of inexpensive firearms coupled with "the appeal of liquor made taverns in the smokeless coalfields the principal sites of gunplay."[52] The combination of alcohol with the rough atmosphere created by the coalfields often resulted in altercations over anything from gambling to such "trivial disagreements as ownership of a pair of shoes."[53] A young Otto Wood found visits to his family in the coalfields exciting and later recalled:

I spent most of my time around the saloon and witnessed several bloody battles between the Hatfields and McCoys. I would not run as other boys did when trouble started but tried to get up close so I could see every movement. The Hatfields noticed that I did not become excited and became attached to me. . . . They made and drank whiskey, gambled, and had a big time generally. I engaged in all of this. They would give me money and play cards with me, always letting me win the game. By the time I was ten years old, I knew the gambling game pretty well. I did not stay with these people all the time, but made an occasional trip to see my mother back in North Carolina.[54]

Though his account is not above the suspicion of embellishment—the Hatfield-McCoy conflict ended in 1889, at least four years before Wood's birth—the coalfields' influence on Wood was validated by his frequent use of the region as a haven during his adulthood.[55]

Not entirely dissimilar to the description that Wood gave in his autobiography, the Hatfields still received attention for committing violent acts within the coalfields throughout the early years of the twentieth century. The battles involved not the McCoys but a series of sporadic attacks between members of the extended family of "Cap" Hatfield, who operated a "blind tiger"—a bar for illicit spirits—in the community of Wharncliffe, Mingo County.[56] In one prominent example from September 1906, "Cap" and his younger brother, Dr. Elias R. Hatfield, settled a personal dispute in a shootout on a stretch of railroad track below Wharncliffe.[57] Elias wounded his older brother with two pistol shots to the chest as they closed on one another from a distance of forty yards.[58] The young Dr. Hatfield, far from an uneducated mountaineer feudist, held a degree from Louisville Medical College.[59] Though Wood may not have given an altogether truthful account of his exposure to the Hatfields, his casting of them as rough yet intelligent people held much more weight and accuracy than other contemporary and often sensationalized descriptions of the infamous family of feudists.

Wood claimed that he worked as a trapper boy in the southern coalfields from the age of thirteen, sometime between 1906 and 1908.[60] Two years later, on the 1910 census, Wood still described himself as a farm laborer—a fact not necessarily contradictory to his earlier account, in which he stated that he frequently moved back and forth between West Virginia and Wilkes.[61] At seventeen, Wood stated that he had become a locomotive fireman on a line for the Norfolk and Western Railway that ran from Bluefield through the coalfields to Williamson, West Virginia, though no sources have emerged to support this claim.[62] Except for a few stories told through oral history, Wood's later teenage years remain a mystery. The small amount of information on this period of his life produced contradictions that Wood never fully addressed in his later writings and interviews.

Most notable among these stories later muddied by Wood's silence involved the loss of his left hand, which occurred when he was eighteen. The handicap, in addition to his noticeable limp, impeded the outlaw's ability to avoid identification by lawmen. Though newspapers popularly blamed a railroad accident, family members, including a cousin, Luther P. Staley, later revealed that Wood had lost his hand while on a trip home to Wilkes County.[63] According to the family's version, the eighteen-year-old Wood "went hunting . . . a quarter mile east of [his mother's] front door he saw that the lid was down on Harrison Parks' rabbit gum. Leaning his shotgun against a bush, he bent down to take the rabbit out of the gum. . . . His shotgun was slipping. . . . He reached for it, too late. . . . The barrel roared. . . . He caught the full barrel load close range in his left hand."[64] The family sent for Dr. R. W. Pegram, who examined Wood's maimed hand in the home of Reverend Jim Majors.[65] Staley, an eyewitness, remembered, "Dr. Pegram said that Otto's hand had to come off," and according to Staley's account Pegram then called for a Dr. Turner, who took Wood's hand off at the wrist.[66] Doctor R. W. Pegram recounted the removal of Wood's hand in 1931, clarifying that he performed the amputation on April 29, 1911.[67] With the loss of his hand, Wood seems to have altogether given up on trying any legitimate occupation—if he had ever considered one at all. From this point forward, the pace of his criminal activities would only accelerate.

In 1926, while in the North Carolina State Prison writing his autobiography, Wood offered a few lines about his early years as a child and young man in the hills of Wilkes County. Wood opined, "I never found any place so dear to me as the little home town in the mountains of Wilkes County. . . . I love the people of Wilkes and am glad to hear of any improvements in the little town of North Wilkesboro."[68] Inhabiting the role of a penitent, reformed prisoner, Wood further stated, "I expected to stay in North Carolina the rest of my life. . . . If I could not stay in Wilkes County, I would stay just as near there as possible."[69] The truth behind this sentiment would eventually lead to Wood's downfall in the winter of 1930.

No matter what weakness Wood felt for the attraction of his home, he suffered no feelings of nostalgia for the hills of Wilkes County or the coalfields of West Virginia. In his mind, these places spawned the criminal activities that he committed as an adult. By his own words, he pleaded the case that he, a victim of poverty and neglect, would have benefited from better conditions at home.

> Looking back to the days of my childhood, I can picture in my mind's eye the conduct of those who were responsible for the life I led. I realize I was restless and irresponsible, but I am loyal and forgiving and pray to God that all will be well with them in the end. I believe that the lives of 75 percent of the criminals had their settings in early environments

of the home circle. Many young people start out in the battle of life with handicaps from which there appears no escape. A child will generally respond to kindness. He will also resent cruelty and neglect. Poverty with love and affection appeals to a child more than luxury without either. Few children I believe have the inclination to leave the right sort of home. They may crave adventure, but love and kindness overcome this desire. Even a hardened criminal responds to kindly treatment.[70]

In one paragraph, Wood summarized the beginnings of his criminal career and constructed the argument on which he would later hinge his appeal for public sympathy. Even as his crimes became more outlandish and his image as a daring criminal solidified—a persona both reviled and admired by those who read about him or encountered him—Wood never forgot the key weapon he had against the world: pity. If people pitied him, they would always be caught unaware, never suspecting his next robbery or his next escape.

CHAPTER 2

OUTLAW OF THE BOONE TRAIL

CARJACKING AND THE WOOD

CRIME FAMILY, 1913–1917

At that time Otto was weaving the threads of life as automobile thief, holder-up of filling stations and general desperado. He was spreading all over Northwestern North Carolina a mortal fear of him as did Jesse James in the years of long ago. Otto must have read the books on the manner of life led by the famous James Brothers for he, like them, loved to ride up and down the Boone trail casting fear in the hearts of officers and others alike. It is said that in some places people looked at the setting sun with fear and trembling because Otto Wood might pass that way.
—*Statesville (NC) Landmark*, November 25, 1926

Otto Wood is said to have only one arm, but from the way he likes auto rides he has only one leg.
—*Twin-City Sentinel* (Winston-Salem, NC), October 5, 1916

One can dodge the law much easier in a car.
—Otto Wood, *Life History*, 1926

SOMETHING WAS NOT RIGHT about "Conductor Wilson" in the Norfolk and Western yards at Graham, Virginia—and the trainmen all knew it. Wilson lingered too long around the freight cars, professing his membership in the Brotherhood of Railway Trainmen to anyone who questioned him. Curiously, when asked the number of his lodge, Wilson failed to answer, vaguely referring to a "Kansas branch," a response that made the railroad men suspicious. Why was a conductor from the Midwest, with neither a train nor any real means of identification, in their railyard? Nearly seven hundred miles away, residents of Clinton, Missouri, recalled the odd appearance of Conductor Wilson two weeks earlier when he arrived on the train from Kansas City in his shirtsleeves, complaining of the loss of his suit and personal effects from a caboose. Now, weeks later in western

Virginia, railroad workers became even more nervous when asking Wilson to repeat his credentials, only to hear a name that, to them, sounded less like "Wilson" and more like "Wood."[1]

Living in the hills of western North Carolina during the late 1910s must have seemed, to those who experienced it, like living in a world on the brink of apocalypse. The onset of warfare on a new, massive industrial scale in Europe called young men away from their homes. In return, a virulent strain of influenza, dubbed "the Spanish flu," emerged from the trenches and spread into homes worldwide, causing an epidemic that hit the rural communities in the foothills and mountains of North Carolina especially hard. In July 1916, weeks of continuous rainfall caused major flooding in the area, exploding aquifers on mountainsides and creating mudslides and flash flooding that claimed lives throughout the region. As a rather symbolic event for the entire period, large sections of the twenty-four-mile flume of the Champion Lumber Company, running from the mountains of Ashe County down to North Wilkesboro, toppled from the slopes, forever destroying what some considered one of the man-made wonders of the Old North State.

Otto Wood looked to his family for strength in an increasingly unstable world. His younger brother Robert Lee Wood, known as "Bob," became, alongside his mother, Ellen, a consistent ally throughout this time. Wood returned home on multiple occasions, each time with a price on his head. Authorities from Tennessee and Virginia sought Wood's capture after a spree of robberies throughout those states—a series of crimes that first reached the attention of the press after thefts occurred along the lines of Norfolk and Western Railway.

On March 27, 1913, Constable Roland of Graham, Tazewell County, Virginia (modern-day Bluefield), arrested one "C. D. Wilson" for breaking into freight cars at the Norfolk and Western yards. Finding receipts from the Brotherhood of Railway Trainmen, Kansas City Lodge, in the man's pockets, the Virginia lawman made calls to Missouri officials and discovered that the real C. D. Wilson, a conductor on the Kansas City Clinton and Springfield Railroad, and several members of his train crew had reported the disappearance of items of clothing two weeks earlier.[2] Railroad detectives following a stream of thefts confirmed that the Wilson arrested in Virginia was Otto H. Wood, by this time known as a "professional robber of freight cars."[3] Wood, under the guise of Wilson, had previously broken into railcars along the lines north of Graham at Switchback, West Virginia. The detectives also attached Wood's name to the theft of a bicycle from Van Lear Brothers, a pharmacy and soda fountain in Roanoke, Virginia. A month after his capture, the circuit court at Tazewell sentenced Wood to two years' hard labor on the convict road force at the Virginia State Penitentiary.[4] Otto later claimed that he worked as a fireman on the Norfolk and Western Railway during this period, maintaining relationships with two women along the rail line, one at Graham, Virginia, and the other at Point Pleasant, West Virginia. Wood even said his Virginia Penitentiary sentence resulted from his abandonment of the girl in Graham, leaving her unmarried and pregnant, incurring the wrath of her father. Close examination of evidence in newspaper reports and prison records suggests that Wood's memories twisted his impersonation of a railroad man and replaced any outline of the crimes he committed for tales of love interests and seductions.[5]

Wood entered the Virginia State Penitentiary on May 10, 1913, assigned to Road Camp 27 in Spotsylvania County, several counties north of the prison's main campus in Richmond.[6] As with his experience on the Iredell chain gang, Wood's physical handicaps—now including the loss of his left hand—convinced prison officials to select him for lighter duties than the hard labor expected of other prisoners. The routine of carrying water to from a nearby spring allowed Wood to slip away from the watchful eye of guards long enough to make his escape only five days after his arrival at the camp. A seemingly unrelated theft of three suitcases from a caboose in the Chesapeake and Ohio Railway's yards in Richmond went unnoticed until a month later, when a patrolman discovered one of the stolen suitcases in a lumberyard. The grip contained striped prison clothes stamped "11522," Wood's prisoner identification number. Police found another piece of the missing luggage in a pawnshop, where Wood, after having exchanged clothing, hawked the suitcase for the fare to leave Richmond.[7]

Arriving back in Wilkes County in July 1913, Otto seemingly made little attempt to keep a low profile. A column in the *North Wilkesboro Hustler* reported his arrest in the Oakwood community at the end of the month and announced Wood's return to Richmond.[8] Whether Wood made it to the Wilkes County jail to await extradition remains unclear, yet he shortly thereafter was once again at large and reappeared in the local news cycle in Wilkes for the next month. Notably, Ellen Wood and Robert Wood faced charges of assault before the Wilkes County Superior Court only a week later. Officials found Ellen not guilty, but Bob Wood's case appears to have continued. It seems possible that these charges against Otto's family were at least in some way related to his escape.[9]

Constable J. P. Shew, a Civil War veteran assigned the policing of the Antioch township, reported his attempt to seize Wood from the house of

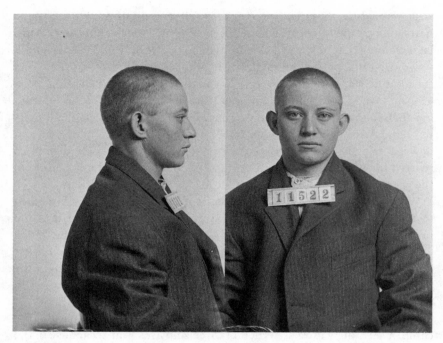

Wood's mugshot, taken around the time he entered the Virginia State
Penitentiary in May 1913. (Courtesy of the Library of Virginia)

Jacob Wood, at the time occupied by Otto and several other young men.
Shew botched the arrest, allowing Wood time to escape outside, where the
young fugitive reemerged at the top of a hill and shouted profanities while
brandishing a pistol. Apparently emboldened by Shew's reticence to pursue
him up the slope, Wood advanced downward toward the elderly constable.
Noticing a shotgun slung over Wood's shoulder, Shew went back down the
road from the house, Wood taunting him as he made his retreat. In the descriptions of the proceedings of Wilkes County Superior Court that featured
Shew's story, court officials argued over the technicalities of the papers demanding Wood's arrest, likely encountering disputes about who would next
find themselves responsible for Wood's capture. In continuation of an earlier case, Bob Wood was also featured in the court dockets for the conceal-
ment of a firearm, a charge he failed to show up for in court.[10]

Authorities in Wilkes thereafter received reports of Wood at the home of
friends in the Brushy Mountains. The *North Wilkesboro Hustler* described
officers cornering Wood on a small farm "at the foot of the Brushies":

Otto has rambled in Virginia, been convicted of stealing, and "hided" it back to Wilkscarolina [a common nickname for Wilkes in this era?]; and only a week ago was spending a night with innocent friends at the foot of the Brushies when observed strolling out before breakfast in the morning at day to the barn of the father of "his girl" to take a toddy from his bottle hidden the night before in the straw after an entertainment in the neighborhood. As a guest he then returned to further impose on the host for his breakfast, but was followed and brought out of the dining [room] a minute later before the eyes of his young lady a prisoner instead of a guest at first declaring that he could not afford socially to go into town with handcuffs; that he had been arrested a thousand times but had never before been so much insulted. Otto is a bad one and there is no telling when he'll get enough lesson to make him stop and be some kind of a man at least.[11]

Whether Otto's protector, "his girl," mentioned in this account, matches any of the names of women later associated with Wood may never be clear. A retrospective on Wood's criminal activities, featured in the November 25, 1926, edition of the *Statesville Landmark*, indicates that around this time Wood began a relationship with Rushey Hayes; they eventually married and had two children. Hayes told reporters that Wood often visited her family's farm in Dellaplane, Wilkes County, but that she and her parents believed he worked as an automobile salesman.[12] Although reporters in 1926 gave Rushey the benefit of the doubt, the amount of news circulating throughout Wilkes during this period concerning Wood's criminal activities makes any ignorance of Wood's background by any Wilkes County family highly suspect.

Prisoner records indicate that Wood returned to the Virginia State Penitentiary a month later, on September 7, 1913. Wood's reentry onto the prison roles indicates additional charges, possibly thefts committed in the weeks before returning to Wilkes. The prison register notes that West Virginia officials in Guyandotte, Cabell County, wanted Wood at the expiration of his Virginia prison term.[13] This locality, near Huntington, was where Wood's older brother, Luther, ran a jitney service. Whether Wood sought refuge with Luther during his escape from authorities is up for speculation. However, Wood's appearance near the home of a family member seems more than just a coincidence.[14]

The Virginia Penitentiary's road camps held Wood for almost a year before he made his second escape from Camp 27 on November 20, 1914.[15] Otto's *Life History* claims he went west during this escape, traveling through the American Southwest on a spree of drinking and gambling. "I wore two big guns . . . was known throughout that part of the country as a tough easterner," Wood recalled, noting that he "was lucky the [he] did not have to kill anybody during the two years [he] remained in the far West."[16] A picture postcard sent to Ellen Wood in December 1914 indicates that Wood did indeed travel to Texas. The photo shows Wood giving the camera a cold-eyed stare, wearing a ten-gallon hat and leveling an antiquated 1860s Colt Army revolver directly at the camera. The image shows that Wood purpose-fully cultivated the image of an old western outlaw. The outdated pistol was clearly a prop, not unlike those still used at "Wild West" and "Old Timey" photo studios at tourist attractions. Wood's pose also appears more than a little influenced by an iconic frame from the 1903 film *The Great Train Robbery*, in which an outlaw shoots his pistol directly into the camera. The inspiration of cowboy literature and films, popular worldwide during this era, for Wood's bandit persona cannot be overstated. A victim of one of Wood's robberies nearly a decade later remarked that Otto and a com-panion shot their guns in the air as almost a pantomime of "a Wild West thriller."[17] Wood claimed to have sojourned throughout the West for two years. However, Wilkes County sources indicate that his travels as western gunslinger—no matter how real or imagined—lasted a little less than a year.

By the end of 1915, Wood reemerged as a car thief in the foothills and mountains of Tennessee and western North Carolina. The increase in the number of automobiles across the United States in this period offered low-hanging fruit for someone with Wood's lawless proclivities. Early auto-mobiles possessed relatively few safeguards for owners to prevent their theft. The Federal Bureau of Investigation details the ease with which cars could be stolen during this era: "In these early days, cars were easy to steal. Few had built-in locks. Ignitions were primitive and easy to hotwire. Vehicle identification numbers didn't exist. Owners often left their automobiles out in the open or parked for hours on busy streets as they went about their days."[18] No doubt with these same factors in mind, Wood wasted no time in shifting his attention from railroads to the highways. With the Bureau of Investigation still a decade and a half from reforms that would combat emerging modern criminals such as Wood, the tracking of stolen auto-mobiles across state lines largely depended on cooperation between re-gional law enforcement agencies. By the early 1920s, Wood became known throughout the Southeast as a serial car thief and highwayman.

While on patrol on November 13, 1915, Salisbury, North Carolina, police chief J. Frank Miller and a fellow officer gave chase to a Ford car recently reported stolen from the front of the home of Statesville local C. E. Ritchie.

Wood dressed as a cowboy in Texas, ca. December 1914.
This grainy, slightly out-of-focus photograph is from a picture
postcard he sent to his mother. (Courtesy of the *Wilkes Record*)

Their pursuit wound through the streets for several blocks before the officers caught the automobile and arrested the driver, "C. H. Staley."[19] Even
though Staley was missing his left hand, the Statesville officers failed
to identify the carjacker as Otto Wood—using an alias probably built by
hybridizing his mother's maiden name with the "C." from "C. D. Wilson"
and the "H." from his middle name, "Harrison." Wood denied stealing
Ritchie's car but admitted knowing that the vehicle was stolen before he
purchased it. Miller also found a watch on Wood's person, engraved "W. K."
The red flags of the engraved watch not matching the initials of Wood's
alias, along with the prisoner's refusal to talk or indicate his origins, led

the officers to (rightly) assume that "C. H. Staley" was guilty of more crimes than just a single car theft.[20] While in jail in Statesville awaiting an appearance before the superior court, Wood told his jailer "he was not in any hurry" to appear before a judge.[21] Traveling to Salisbury to retrieve his car, C. E. Ritchie gave the officers a $100 reward, an amount he previously posted for its safe return.[22]

Otto Wood managed to convince officers of his identity as "C. H. Staley" over the three-month period of his imprisonment in Statesville. In the February 1916, "Staley" took the stand as a witness for the state in the case of Houston Overcash, an Iredell County farmer accused of murdering his estranged wife with a shotgun.[23] Wood's evidence, in part, turned the trial against Overcash, alleging that the murder suspect took him in confidence while the two were in jail together. According to Wood's testimony, Overcash told of plans to plead insanity if alibis for his whereabouts on the night of the murder failed. Overcash, in turn, took the stand to deny ever talking with his fellow inmate.[24] The trial culminated with Overcash pleading guilty to second-degree murder, resulting in a sentence of thirty years in the North Carolina State Prison.[25] Wood faced his own trial shortly thereafter and received six months' hard labor, returning him once again to the Iredell County chain gang. Wood broke from the chain gang shortly after his arrival and seems to have largely disappeared, perhaps lining up with one of many instances of him traveling in western states under an alias.[26]

In the fall of 1916, a stream of car thefts throughout the Piedmont and northwestern counties of North Carolina announced Wood's return home. In late September, Special Officer Edward W. Oliver, a detective for the Southern Railway, traveled north from Winston-Salem alongside Winston resident Pinkney O. Leak. In search of Leak's touring car, stolen a few days earlier, the pair followed a series of leads first to Elkin and then southwest to North Wilkesboro. After two days in the area, on September 26, the pair found Leak's car in a vacant lot just outside of town. Special Officer Oliver seems to have kept in constant communication with regional authorities concerning reports of stolen cars, collecting information at any stops with telephone or telegraph stations as they searched for Leak's automobile.[27] Recovering the stolen vehicle, Leak and Oliver headed back to Elkin from North Wilkesboro. Traveling east, they met an Overland car that Oliver recognized as matching the description of one listed as missing in Tennessee. Stopping and searching the Overland, Oliver found tools belonging to Leak's touring car in the trunk. Now building a case around a ring of automobile thefts, Oliver had the driver, Frank Staley, a cousin of Wood's family, arrested and escorted back to North Wilkesboro. Oliver later discovered that the car, thought to have been stolen in Tennessee, belonged to the owner of gas company in Kenova, West Virginia. Shortly after Staley's arrest, a brown Buick passed the duo's car. On entering the town of Elkin, the police chief informed Leak and Oliver of a stolen Buick belonging to Charles Hauser of High Point. The pair immediately recognized the vehicle as the one that passed by shortly after Staley's arrest.[28]

The Elkin police notified their counterparts in North Wilkesboro to keep watch for the stolen Buick, also wiring authorities in High Point, who responded by immediately dispatching Special Officer David Yow and an Officer Carroll north to identify and assist in the capture of the stolen car. That afternoon, Chief of Police Hart of North Wilkesboro organized volunteers into a posse to capture the Buick and its driver somewhere on the border of town. Sightings of the automobile near Wood's home section of Dellaplane, six miles east of North Wilkesboro, prompted lawmen to gather in that area. Watching the stolen car emerge from what sources described as an "obscure side road," the armed group made their move and advanced on the Buick. Before the officers could close in, Otto and Bob Wood leaped out of the car and rushed toward a nearby tree line. As other deputies pursued the outlaw brothers, one policeman ran to stop the car as it careened away with a woman and child still inside.[29] Based on Rushey Haye's 1926 interview, her marriage to Wood places her and one of her children as the most probable occupants of Hauser's Buick during this incident.[30]

The High Point officers, assisted by two Wilkes County men, W. A. McNeil and James Phillips, again cornered the Wood brothers in Dellaplane on September 27. Though they captured the younger Wood, the arresting officers failed to bring in Otto, who held the lawmen off with a pistol and fled with a companion reported as "his wife or paramour"—language once again pointing to Rushey Hayes.[31] Several news columns erroneously featured a report of Otto Wood's capture, perhaps confusing him with his younger brother. Other columns noted that Officer Carroll telegraphed his superiors that Otto Wood had escaped. The captured members of the gang were transported to jail in High Point, where officials showed a surprising amount of leniency toward Bob Wood. The press outlined the general belief among police and locals that Bob had played only a minor role in the string of car thefts. Officers also detained another young Wilkes County man, Otho Johnson, as part of the ring, but acknowledged that he, like Bob, probably only helped move the cars, naming Frank Staley and Otto as the main culprits.[32]

As patrols fanned out around Wilkes looking for the elder Wood, authorities in High Point questioned Frank Staley on his involvement in the recent spree of thefts. With information from McNeill and Phillips who assisted in the arrest, officials prepared to place Staley and Bob Wood on trial. "Staley is a young fellow of good parentage," wrote one reporter covering the case, noting that "this is first trouble he was ever in."[33] Staley confessed to having rendezvoused with Otto in Winston-Salem the previous morning, where he agreed to drive the Overland stolen by Wood to North Wilkesboro. Neighbors of Charles Hauser in High Point reported seeing a group of men breaking into Hauser's garage and rolling his car out into the street at around the same time as Staley's affirmed meeting with Wood. Additionally, Otto's older brother, James, informed police that the gang tried to sell him Hauser's automobile for $90 on the day of its theft. As stories stacked up concerning the band of robbers, authorities pinpointed a Buick belonging to Mrs. J. R. Reitzel, missing from the town's Main Street since September 24, as Wood's new ride. This report was soon complicated by Special Officer E. W. Oliver, still on the case, who confirmed the theft of two more automobiles earlier in the week, a Ford in Statesville and another car of an unidentified make in Greensboro.[34]

Otto Wood hardly laid low while Frank Staley and Bob Wood spent their first evening in jail, waiting to appear before the court in High Point the next morning. Late that night, Otto backtracked to North Wilkesboro to steal yet another Buick, this one belonging to Clem Wrenn, a cashier at a local bank. Several witnesses spotted a 1915 Buick leaving the town headed south around three in morning on September 28, speculating Wood's destination as the Iredell County line. Officers discovered the scene of a break-in at Jenkins' Hardware Store the next morning in downtown North Wilkesboro, evidenced by a shattered rear window and twisted security bars. In some disturbingly haphazard record keeping, the store offered an estimate of the arsenal removed from their shelves, which included "10 revolvers, 25 or 30 knives, two breech-loading and one automatic shot gun [sic] and a Remington rifle . . . and much ammunition." Chief of Police Hart of North Wilkesboro, fearing the worst-case scenario, sent word to Chief Gray of High Point to prepare to defend the jail there against "any armed invasion that might be made to get three men now under arrest." Though not unwarranted in his fears of Wood attempting to free his compatriots, Hart probably seriously misjudged Wood's character. If past criminal activities constituted any pattern, Wood—at least at this point in his life—more likely intended to sell most of the guns at some location along his path, evading police rather than risking a full-on shootout with them.[35]

Justices of the Wilkes County Superior Court declared Wood an outlaw, placing a $50 reward on his head—dead or alive.[36] This pronouncement

constituted the first time Wood was officially deemed an "outlaw." Although
the severity of the term has lost much of its punch in modern language,
anyone "outlawed" during this period literally existed outside the law's
protection. The outlawry statute of North Carolina, based on fugitive slave
laws from the nineteenth century, was harsh in its distribution of justice.
Historian Kevin Young states that this designation practically sanctioned
murder, in that anyone who killed someone declared an outlaw would face
no repercussions, as long as they could make the case that the person outlawed had resisted or tried to flee after being ordered to surrender.[37]

With Wood remaining at large, the press turned to reciting Otto's known
history as a childhood criminal. A column in the *Charlotte Observer* recounted that as a child Wood "was sentenced to a hospital for treatment
[presumably for his clubbed foot] and a purse of about $25 made up to pay
his expenses," a mistake that only benefited his current "profession."[38]
Newspapers also paid attention to the reaction of people in North Wilkesboro to Wood's carjacking spree. A story from North Wilkesboro gave an account of defensive actions taken by locals in expectation of Wood's return:
"Automobile owners are taking every precaution to avoid losing their cars,
some of them sleeping in their garages, while others take other precautions.
One of Otto's brothers [James Wood] lives here in town and is among car
owners who don't want to take the risk, and it was noticed last night he
took one wheel off his car to render it unavailable for the purpose it is supposed Otto would want one. He is not in sympathy with his brother's wild
career, and is a good citizen."[39] A similar column printed in the *Greensboro
Daily News* noted that "the excitement over the influx of stolen automobiles
has subsided very little."[40] Even with the known members of Wood's gang
behind bars, locals seemingly recognized Otto as the expert joyrider from
among the bunch.

By the second week of October 1916, High Point residents offered their
own rewards for Wood's capture, amounting to the sum of $125. Mrs. Reit-
zel, still hoping to recover her Buick, offered $100 of the reward. Guilford
County provided an additional $20 for Wood's capture, and High Point chief
of police C. L. Gray offered $5 from his own pocket.[41] A wanted poster fea-
turing Wood's mugshot from the Virginia State Penitentiary was printed
in the local newspaper and circulated across the Piedmont and mountain
counties of North Carolina. The reward advertisement profiled Wood's
physical appearance, pointing out his missing hand and clubbed foot. "He
walks slightly on tip-toe on one foot," the poster noted, adding, "He leans
well forward on the steering wheel when driving an automobile to hide his
stub wrist." The description of Wood also stated that he often traveled in

the company of his wife.[42] The *High Point Review*, expanding on a piece built around the "mountain-rube-comes-to-town" stereotype, asked a livestock trader from Sparta, Alleghany County, North Carolina, his opinion on Otto Wood's crimes and the reward offered for his capture. Having traveled through scenes of destruction caused by the Great Flood of July 1916, the High Point journalist confidently claimed he had met the mountaineer who stood a good chance of being at the center of the next great western North Carolina news story. "You bet [the man from Sparta] will land Wood if given half a chance," bragged the High Point columnist, "'cause he knows every pig path in a radius of 100 miles and he has been on scouting parties before."[43]

Disappointing the Sparta livestock trader and others in the North Carolina Piedmont, Wood's capture occurred well outside the hundred-mile radius. The Buick stolen from Clem Wrenn in North Wilkesboro turned up in a garage in Chattanooga, Tennessee, in late October. Wood sold the car and immediately proceeded to steal another, this one belonging to a railroader working the Southern Railway line between Cincinnati and Chattanooga.[44] Police arrested Wood in the vehicle farther north, on the Cumberland Plateau in Pine Knot, Kentucky. Bringing Wood back to Chattanooga for trial, officers there forwarded news of Wood's capture to Southern Railway's Special Officer Oliver in Winston-Salem and to Chief of Police Gray in High Point.[45]

Perhaps giving Wood some small piece of good news and disappointing lawmen in Tennessee, Chief Gray removed the $125 reward placed on Wood's head for stealing Mrs. Reitzel's car. The chief informed the press on October 21 that the unrelated theft had been traced to Clay Moore, son of a local contractor and described by the *High Point Enterprise* as "one of High Point's most respected citizens." Moore, a twenty-two-year-old man who had had a clean record up to this point, stole clothing from a store in High Point and then lifted Reitzel's automobile at around the same time that the Wood gang stole Hauser's. The young man then drove the car north, stealing several other cars along the way, until police captured him in Reading, Pennsylvania.[46]

Simultaneous to Moore's capture, officials in Tennessee and North Carolina clashed over Wood's custody. While Special Agent Oliver lobbied for Wood's return to face the superior court in Greensboro, the municipal court in Chattanooga proceeded to put Wood on trial for the car theft committed in Tennessee. Cold-shouldering Oliver, the Tennessee authorities eventually got back in touch to let their North Carolina counterparts know that Wood was not returning to face trial in their state until the completion of his sentence in Tennessee.[47] Sentenced to the Tennessee State Penitentiary, Otto arrived there on December 3, 1916. Curiously, his entry includes a request to notify "Mrs. Sarah Wood of Chattanooga, Tennessee" of his incarceration.[48] Whether this "Sarah Wood" was a relative, a person in a relationship with Wood, or even a real person at all, remains unclear. Wood stayed confined in Nashville for nearly half a year before once again breaking from his captivity in May 1917.[49] No contemporary news accounts or passages from Wood's *Life History* provide any solid details on exactly how the Wood managed this escape from the stockade in Nashville.

North Carolina newspapers covered Wood's return to Wilkes County in June 1917, a homecoming announced by the disappearance of a Ford car.[50] On the night of June 2, Wilkes County sheriff W. D. Woodruff, alongside three deputies, followed a lead to the home of Wood's mother. The Wilkes County man providing the tip claimed to have run into Wood on the road in Dellaplane the previous night. The officers lay in wait throughout the night and captured Wood the next morning as he tried to climb into a car outside his mother's house.[51] Hauled to jail in Wilkesboro, Wood completed paperwork for the recent draft while in his cell two days later. Filling out the section of the form asking for "present trade," Wood (or the officers filling out the form for him) listed himself as "in jail awaiting release to Tennessee Penitentiary."[52] Wood's name appeared in local news alongside those of other Wilkes County men registered for the draft.[53]

While awaiting his extradition to Tennessee, Wood took time to construct the first of many letters to the public, initially published in the *Wilkes Journal-Patriot* and reprinted in other regional papers. The letter placed the blame for Wood's current criminal activities on Wilkes County's people.

> To whom it may concern:
>
> I guess the people of the state of North Carolina and perhaps many of other states, have seen an account of the writer—Otto H. Wood—and have often wondered what kind of a man he could be. It is true, ladies and gentlemen, I have been a noted man around the world. I have been in a number of prisons and I am in one at this time, but I would like to say to some of the citizens of Wilkes county that they are to blame for what I am today. It seemed they were all down on me and at the age of ten years I left my home and went to St. Louis, Mo. I was gone three months and I saw the worst of the world and I haven't ever stayed at home to amount to anything. I ran around till the age of eighteen when I went to firing for the Norfolk and Western Railway Company and worked something over two years. I came home on a visit

and happened to [have] the misfortune shooting my left fingers off and then I was up against it. I tried to make good, but the people seemed like they could not let me alone, so I left home and I got in a number of places, and I got in so bad I did not care. I then went to Bramwell, W. Va. Where I was married and started a business. But after I was married and was trying to make good they go after me again and I had to leave there. Well, I came back to the state of North Carolina and they got after me again, so I decided that I never would try to make good any more. I went to Chattanooga, Tenn. with my wife and I got in bad there. November 3 I was tried and sentenced for three to ten years. I was made a trusty [*sic*], but later I was put under the gun and I made my escape again but was captured in Dellaplane, Wilkes county, N. C. I admit I haven't done right, but by the help of some good people I think I can make good yet, so I hope that the people will take this into consideration and give me a chance again. If they will only give me a little chance I will make a show for myself. So I will ask the people of Wilkes county to do something for me, for I am willing to be made a law-abiding citizen of the state, as I have a wife and a mother who is getting old, both of whom I love and I am willing to accept any offer. So I hope the good people will think it over.

Thanking the editor for a little space in the Patriot

OTTO HARRISON WOOD.[54]

Here Wood selectively left out his time in the Virginia State Penitentiary, opting instead to claim that he worked for the railroad during that period of his life. Notably, this letter constitutes the only time Wood gave anything close to an accurate story of how he lost his left hand—in all future accounts he replaced it with a vague story of a railroad accident. Wilkes County residents, aware of the truth surrounding Wood's recent history, probably recognized many of the falsehoods in Wood's letter.

In a bizarre decision, after constructing a fairly cogent plea for clemency (albeit one not without self-aggrandizing storytelling) Wood decided to half-jokingly sweeten the deal. In a postscript attached to the letter, the noted carjacker addressed his potential use in the current war brewing in Europe:

P.S.—Just a word about the war. Gentlemen, it seems that the citizens of the United States are about to get into a war with Germany. I will make the suggestion that the quickest way that we can get out of Germany is to send me to Germany and let me capture the Kaiser and his automobile in Germany. I had started one time and I met my friend Sewel

Webster in Dellaplane and I mistook him for a friend. I thought he was going with me, but he mistook me for the Kaiser and brought me and my car to Wilkesboro. I haven't seen Mr. Webster since he found out his mistake but I suppose he is in a hospital suffering from a nervous shock, tho [sic] he was pretty well prepared and had a double-barreled shotgun with both hammers back.

Gentlemen, in regard to Mr. Clem Wrenn's car that was taken by the so-called Otto H. Wood. Some one borrowed my car and I borrowed Mr. Wrenn's car, but was the best fellow. I returned Mr. Wrenn's car in good shape. He said his car was worth $500 more when got it back so I didn't do him any injurey [sic] at all.

OTTO H. WOOD
Wilkesboro, N. C., June 6, 1917.[55]

This addition to Wood's appeal for sympathy seems largely to have undercut any small hope of legitimizing his case to his fellow North Carolinians. "Send Him Over," joked one column. "We'll bet on Wood getting the automobile and come as near getting the Kaiser as anyone."[56] To Wood's credit, a small contingent of American soldiers—composed mainly of National Guardsmen from Tennessee—attempted a similar plan to kidnap Kaiser Wilhelm II from a castle in the Netherlands nearly two years later.[57]

On sending Wood back to the Tennessee Penitentiary, Wilkes County residents were liable to have to breathed a collective sigh of relief. Over the course of four years, Wood had returned repeatedly, creating havoc in his home county. His antics led authorities to legally declare him an outlaw. Now, back behind the walls of the penitentiary in Nashville, he was no longer their concern. Despite Wood's capture and extradition, some residents must have wondered when he would next reemerge to haunt his home section of Dellaplane. True to form, Wood could not leave them in suspense for long and would reappear in less than year. This time he would return to engage in the transporting what was becoming the county's chief underground commodity: moonshine whiskey.

CHAPTER 3

THE MOUNTAINS WERE THE SAFEST PLACE

OTTO WOOD, BLOCKADER AND

HIGHWAYMAN, 1918–1923

Men who defy the law must be punished. A new day has dawned.
Laxity toward law enforcement has gone long enough, now the
people are getting their eyes open to see what a monster the liquor
traffic is.
—"Talks by Rev. W. F. Staley," *Carter's Weekly*
  (North Wilkesboro, NC), January 9, 1920

For failure to register [a] still $500 penalty, fine of between $100 and
$1,000 and imprisonment of between one month and two years;
for making liquor in a community where it is prohibited by local
or State laws, tax of $1,000; for violation [of] war-time prohibition
$1,000 fine or one year imprisonment or both; for making a whiskey
mash or a beer, fine of between $500 and $5,000 and imprisonment
of between six months and three years.
—"Warn Liquor-Makers," *North Wilkesboro (NC) Hustler*,
  April 28, 1919

The mountains were the safest place for me to live; so me and the
girl made whiskey. . . . I made good money at this.
—Otto Wood, *Life History*, 1926

THE STRANGER WAS SOMEWHERE out in the woods, and Jack
Cowan peered through the windshield, the headlights of his car
pulling shadows from the trees. The young man knew that something was wrong with his companion, the man he had picked up along
the roadside several hours ago. Cowan drove a jitney for his father's company, riding passengers to locations between Winston-Salem and Statesville, North Carolina. Tonight's passenger, however, was not a paying cus-
tomer and had emerged suddenly from the darkness of the roadside just
before midnight. The man flagged down Cowan's jitney, complaining of a

broken-down car full of passengers waiting somewhere out on the highway. As Cowan drove toward Winston-Salem, the stranger's story changed and the man demanded that they pull into a clearing in the woods on the side of the road. The stranger said something about hauling liquor and finding the man he left to guard a carload of whiskey out in the woods. A few hours later, Cowan walked into the Winston-Salem Police Headquarters to report the theft of his father's car. While Cowan told his story of the robbery, police laid on a table photographs of criminals at large in North Carolina. Cowan immediately recognized a face as the same one that appeared from trees into his headlights: a serial carjacker from Wilkes County named Otto Wood.[1]

During the three years between 1918 and 1921, Otto Wood circulated through the cellblocks of three state penitentiaries across the South and Midwest. With his reputation as a car thief already established in North Carolina and neighboring states, his criminal activities during this period often aligned with the routes of illicit liquor traffic, a network booming due to the onset of regional and then national prohibition of alcohol. Wilkes County was gradually establishing itself as an epicenter of liquor production, with skilled drivers known as "blockaders" hauling booze to Winston-Salem. From this southern city, the liquor was dispersed to far-flung urban areas in the Northeast and Midwest. Wood's participation in blockading would link him to his home county for much of this early era of Prohibition. The strengths of these bonds to home would eventually be tested by personal tragedy and the severance of his closest familial tie to the hills of western North Carolina.

Wood made his second break from the Tennessee State Penitentiary on the afternoon of April 27, 1918.[2] Putting to work his previous experience of breaking into railroad cars, Wood squirreled inside a freight car loaded to leave the prison grounds and rode the rails out of the stockade.[3] Wood recalled in his *Life History* that he chose a large dry-goods box as his hiding place and was only discovered by officers after trying to exit the car outside the prison grounds. His account of this escape offers vivid descriptions of a nighttime manhunt, hearing the yelps of hounds pursuing him in the distance and watching officers' lanterns approach in the dark. Wood claimed he covered much of the distance away from the lawmen on a horse stolen from a local farmstead before he dismounted and continued on foot through a section of woods.[4] No contemporary sources contradict Wood's account, and, if anything, he seems to have underestimated the distance of his run, describing his capture as occurring some forty miles from Nashville. After a two-day run, officers captured Wood on April 29 in Cowan, Tennessee, a small town over eighty miles south of the capital, near the Alabama state line.[5]

Dispatching an officer to take Wood back to the penitentiary, the Cowan authorities sent Wood to Nashville by train. Arriving at Union Station, Nashville's cavernous, cathedral-esque rail hub, Wood took the opportunity to lose his guard and disappear in the bustling atmosphere of the station.[6] Wood later recounted how he managed to escape: "[The Cowan officers] selected a big man, about six feet three inches . . . 250 pounds, to take me back to prison. Someone suggested that he better tie my hands. He did not think this necessary. . . . As we were leaving the train I give him what is known as a 'rabbit punch' to the back of his neck, . . . I did not stay to investigate but made a dash for the railroad yards."[7] Wood then described how he broke into a caboose and found the clothes and effects of a flagman. Exchanging his prison clothes for the flagman's overhauls, Wood smeared his face with grease and carried a lantern, pretending to take part in the search as officers fanned out through the railyard. He then jumped on a train, which took him to "Hoptown" (regional slang for Hopkinsville, Kentucky). Wood remembered that he narrowly missed catching a bullet from the guns of two Hopkinsville officers who tried to arrest him and, by some means, managed to head toward Welch, McDowell County, West Virginia.[8] Contemporary news sources only vaguely outline Wood's escape, but his description of impersonating a railroader seems to validate at least a portion of this story, calling back to reports of his masquerading as Conductor Wilson in Virginia several years earlier.

Wilkes County officials, fearing that Wood's return to the area was inevitable, circulated a reward poster featuring the bandit's photograph in May 1918.[9] Although the amount offered for Wood's arrest on this occasion seems obscured in the extant records, this reward was in addition to previous charges and fines leveled by the state of North Carolina against Otto and Bob Wood, appearing in North Wilkesboro court dockets in January 1918.[10] In Otto's case, the charges likely carried over from his time in Wilkes during the summer and fall of 1917. Aside from whatever offenses brought his name into the local news, Robert Wood was also busy in more romantic pursuits. In June 1918, Bob married nineteen-year-old Celia Byrd of Elkin, North Carolina.[11] Celia would later become a dependable ally for Otto, helping him evade North Carolina authorities in the late 1920s.

Spending several months around southern West Virginia, Wood was picked up for car theft by officers in McDowell County. During his arrest

"C. H. Moore," mugshot from the West Virginia State
Penitentiary, ca. 1918, reprinted in *Master Detective*
magazine, 1933. (Author's collection)

Wood gave his name as "C. H. Moore," leading West Virginia officials to erroneously cite "Woods" as his alias.[12] Given his proclivity for reading papers
regarding his own crimes, Wood presumably borrowed this name from Clay
Moore, the young man who committed robberies in Winston-Salem simultaneous to Wood's carjacking spree in 1916.[13] "Authorities [in West Virginia]
held a warrant against me for taking an automobile on which only part of
the purchase price had been paid," Wood stated in his *Life History*: "The
judge told me the five year sentence was not for the automobile trouble, but
largely on account of my past record."[14] In handing down the five-year sentence, sending Wood to the West Virginia State Penitentiary at Moundsville,
the court probably took into account the previous charges against Wood
farther north, in Cabell County, from 1913.[15]

Arriving in Moundsville on September 5, 1918, Wood almost immediately began plans to escape from the catacomb of cellblocks inside the massive, gothic sandstone building.[16] Key to Wood's plans was James Borders, a twenty-seven-year-old former coal miner from Nolan, Mingo County, West Virginia. Borders had arrived in Moundsville two years earlier, sentenced to eighteen years for the murder of his brother-in-law.[17] Likely due to Wood's childhood connections to southern West Virginia—especially the coal camp at Vulcan, next to Borders's hometown—the two young men quickly took each other in confidence. Wood later recalled the plan hatched by the pair as a desperate venture, something akin to "trying to break the Hindenburg Line in time of battle."[18] Borders and Wood made their break at around three in the morning on January 9, 1919, scaling the prison walls under the cover of a snowstorm.[19] By Wood's account, the weather allowed the pair to safely scale the walls with ladders, without attracting the attention of guards armed with the man-killing firepower of .30-.30 Winchester rifles. The fugitives then followed the Ohio River through three days of intense cold, subsisting under a rock cliff for a short period before turning south toward Huntington.[20]

Accounts of the escape made front-page news in West Virginia and western Pennsylvania newspapers, most of the coverage paralleling the details later outlined by Wood. Several reports mentioned that the escapees made use of a ladder sourced from outside the prison grounds. These narratives also noted that the men shed their prison clothes soon after scaling the wall; the guards likely used the discarded clothes to give their bloodhounds a scent to track the fugitives.[21] The details surrounding the break suggest that someone within the prison, or living and working near the prison grounds, aided Wood and Borders, providing the ladder and leaving clothes for them near the wall. The bloodhounds tracked the fugitives to a wooded area on the outskirts of Moundsville on the banks of the Ohio River before losing their scent.[22]

Within a week, the prison officials at Moundsville contacted police and press in North Carolina, warning them to keep watch for C. H. Moore, alias "Woods." The *Winston-Salem Journal* revealed Moore's true identity, sending a notice that readers should protect their automobiles while reciting the details of Otto Wood's carjacking spree in Winston during the fall of 1916. "It is alleged that Woods [sic] has said that no prison has yet been built that will hold him for any length of time," the article claimed, adding, "Up to this time the boast seems to be true."[23] The Winston reporter also reprinted a letter sent by Moundsville's warden, Joseph Z. Terrell, commenting on the physical traits and personalities of the escaped prisoners:

Enclosed are pictures and descriptions of [the] murderer and auto thief who escaped. . . .

James Borden [*sic*], serial number 9672, is a mountaineer, born on the border of West Virginia and Kentucky, and is known as a crack shot with a revolver or rifle. He was sent from Mingo County, W.Va., July 22, 1916, to serve 18 years for murder committed in the wilds of Mingo. He is a tall, raw-boned mountaineer, with clear blue eyes and wavy brown hair. He has a very meager education and should not be hard to locate, as he is inexperienced in traveling and it is known that Moore [Wood] intends to shake him at his first opportunity.

The other man, C. H. Moore, alias C. H. Woods, serial number 10347, noted auto thief sent from McDowell County, W.Va., September 5, 1918, for five years for grand larceny. He was the brains of the get-away and used Borden [*sic*] as a tool to gain his freedom. Moore is a cripple. He has his left hand off at the wrist and has a very badly smashed foot which causes him to limp and at first appearance one would think one leg was shorter than the other. He keeps the stub of his left arm in his pocket nearly all the time and walks very erect. His criminal history dates back ten years and he is known to the officers of the law as one of the most daring auto thiefs [*sic*] in the country. He is likely to be found around machinery, river fronts, or boats. He has relatives living in Winston-Salem.

There is a $50 reward for each of these men.[24]

Despite nearly making a dime-novel mountaineer of Borders and misreporting the source of Wood's limp, Terrell's letter provides one of the earliest accurate physical descriptions of Wood. The illusion of a shortened leg when walking and the left hand held firmly in a pocket would continually be used to profile and identify Wood in subsequent years. Wood's treatment of Borders as an accomplice—Moundsville officials' acknowledgement of his intent to lose the West Virginian at the first opportunity—falls largely in line with his interaction with future criminal partners. Meeting Terrell's expectations, Wood left the sharpshooting coal miner to fend for himself. Officers cornered James Borders in the mountains near Kenova, Wayne County, West Virginia, in late February 1919 and sent him back to Moundsville. The search continued for Otto Wood.[25]

Otto parted ways with Borders almost immediately after breaking from Moundsville, heading south to western North Carolina and Wilkes County. Whatever hopes Wood had of a happy homecoming and of finding a place to lay low were undoubtedly quashed as he returned to find his home community suffering under the shadow of the Spanish flu. The disease, which terrorized the world in the wake of World War I, hit the people of the mountains and foothills of the Blue Ridge with a vengeance in the fall and winter of 1919. Wood arrived in Wilkes just in time to see his closest partner in crime, his younger brother, Bob, taking his last breaths. Bob, like many other victims of the disease, drowned in his own fluids as the pneumonia that inevitably followed the flu coated his lungs.[26] Perhaps not emotionally equipped to mention Bob's death, in his *Life History* Wood remembered this period as a time when he helped his neighbors battle the epidemic: "When I got back to North Carolina I found many people were dying of influenza. The disease was raging everywhere. I was about the only one able to nurse the sick folks and the people were glad to have me around."[27] Robert Wood's death in the early morning hours of January 30, 1919, brought the Wood family together for a brief period. Otto served as the informant for his brother's death certificate, cryptically noting his address as "West Virginia."[28] Luther and Ellen Wood, visiting her son in Huntington, West Virginia, arrived in North Wilkesboro for the burial, a day after Bob's death.[29]

While the Spanish flu visibly destroyed lives and families in western North Carolina, politicians, newspapers, law enforcement officials, and religious figures all commented on an equally destructive menace in the region—the distilling and distribution of moonshine liquor. Since the ratification of statewide prohibition of alcohol in North Carolina in 1908, the production and consumption of whiskey had spiked among Carolinians.[30] Wood's return to Wilkes County in the early days of 1919 coincided with the ratification of nationwide prohibition under the Volstead Act. Writing about Franklin County, Virginia, later Wilkes County's chief challenger for the title of "moonshine capital of the world," historian Charles D. Thompson Jr. points out that economic stresses on rural communities after the close of World War I only fueled production of illegal liquor. Thompson notes that instead of reinforcing a moral good by removing taxed liquor, the lawmakers behind Prohibition inadvertently "created new channels for profiteering, new avenues for running illegal liquor across state lines, and new ways for people to cheat the government."[31] The opportunities for financial gain, travel, and thrill-seeking offered by this burgeoning underground industry appealed to Otto Wood for obvious reasons.

Evidencing the wide range of the liquor trafficking emanating from Wilkes County, Wood's name appeared in the court dockets of Nashville, Tennessee, in February 1919. *The Tennessean* reported that "C. O. alias Otto Wood" failed to appear in court on charges of "tippling and storage."[32] Wood's case fell alongside those of other men facing jail time and fines for

a host of liquor-related offenses, most involving the production and distribution of alcohol as well as the carrying of firearms.[33] That same month,
Wood's name arose in a list of cases before the Wilkes County Superior
Court, likely for similar offenses.[34] Ellen Wood's name was also listed on the
same docket for unspecified charges.[35]

Throughout the early months of 1919, the *North Wilkesboro Hustler* featured stories on the destruction of stills, arrests of respected community
members involved in the liquor trade, and reports of violence resulting from
liquor trafficking.[36] "There is much said about 'blocking' [another term for
blockading] in Wilkes last year," one report acknowledged. "Persons are
said to have piled up little life-time fortunes for high priced liquor."[37] Wood
later claimed that regular hauls to Winston-Salem provided him with the
beginnings of one such fortune. "[The liquor] was sold for $20 a gallon
wholesale," Wood recalled. "One hundred gallons in Winston would net
me $1,100."[38] Wood stated that living in the mountains near North Wilkes-
boro and engaging in the blockading of liquor afforded him a network that
allowed some degree of safety. He also claimed that a new partner—"a girl
who proved to be such a great pal"—helped him in making moonshine.[39]
Though Wood never divulged this partner's identity, this "girl" could be
Rushey Hayes, who took "Wood" as a last name around this time and later
named him as the father of her child delivered sometime around January
1919.[40] The timing and circumstances also point to the possibility that the
"girl" was Celia Byrd, the widow of Bob Wood. Wood and Byrd's later romantic connections, detailed in the press in the late 1920s, reaffirm that the two
probably began a relationship during this period.

Perhaps emboldened by the wealth afforded by his blockading ventures,
or banking on good graces earned for aiding neighbors afflicted with the
Spanish flu, Otto decided to make his return to Wilkes County known publicly in mid-May 1919. Seemingly little concerned by the fact that he was a
known fugitive and wanted by authorities in West Virginia, Tennessee, and
Virginia, Wood embarked on a decidedly unsubtle tour of the county in a
stolen Buick. Wood's public homecoming even warranted a column in the
local paper: the *North Wilkesboro Hustler* described him as the "center of
attraction" wherever his car stopped.[41] The story on Wood's arrival in North
Wilkesboro on May 14, 1919, appeared with other items in the "Local News
in Town and County" section, which, alongside continued reports of moonshining, included such pedestrian stories as a notice for a community fair, a
description of a horse trade, and reports of a particularly virulent toothache
experienced by a former Wilkes resident. "[Wood] says he has come home to
stay and make good," the *Hustler* reported. "He knows he has done wrong

and now wishes to right himself." Making no mention of the escape from West Virginia, the column closed by noting that Wood had taken up residence with his mother in Dellaplane.[42]

That Friday night, newly elected North Wilkesboro chief of police Golston Smith cornered Wood in a garage.[43] With several stolen Fords and Buicks surrounding him, Wood protested to Smith and the other arresting officers, declaring the purity of his intentions in returning home. "Pistols were found on his person," noted one skeptical local reporter describing Wood's capture, "yet he asks the good people to give him a chance to make good."[44] Detained in the Wilkes County jail for a week, Otto left his home county again on the morning of May 20, 1919, this time accompanied by an officer from the West Virginia Penitentiary.[45]

Wood later commended the kindness of Captain of the Guard E. W. Athey, who escorted him back to Moundsville. By Wood's recollection, Athey allowed "the girl"—presumably the same one who helped Wood make liquor—to accompany them on their journey. The trio traveled to Roanoke, Virginia, where, per Wood, Athey also allowed Otto to stay in a hotel if he promised not to try to escape. Wood also claimed to have turned in a gun that he planned to use to intimidate Athey and make his escape. Athey, moved by this gesture, promised to intercede on Wood's behalf when they reached Moundsville. In Wood's account, the prison officials met on his return and agreed to give him a pardon, contacting West Virginia governor John J. Cornwell and officials in Tennessee and Virginia.[46]

The pardon extended to Wood was probably not as immediate, or as focused on him, as portrayed in his *Life History*. The backlash over harsh sentences under Prohibition laws, coupled with press reports on the revolting conditions of West Virginia's prison road camps and the antiquated facilities at Moundsville, prompted a mass wave of appeals for parole.[47] Under the heading "Fears State Disgrace," one West Virginia reporter responded to accounts of poor sanitation, chaining of prisoners, and men serving long sentences on offenses as minor as "selling a pint of liquor." The columnist worried that West Virginia "has been brought in the limelight so often [on prison issues] that I feel we have suffered material injury because of things published against us."[48] Wood's background in liquor trafficking (and stealing cars for the purposes of hauling liquor) more than likely benefited him in this instance, making him one of the candidates for leniency. Despite the pardons offered for minor liquor offenses and larcenies in West Virginia, the Tennessee State Penitentiary requested Wood's return to serve the duration of his term there. Wood rejoined the convict ranks at the penitentiary in Nashville, Tennessee on January 17, 1920. A note in the prison registry next to this date states, "Court and [Attorney] General recommend that he serve maximum sentence."[49] The entry marking Wood's projected release date shows signs of multiple redactions and updates, with the final release date fixed as June 2, 1926.[50]

The Tennessee Penitentiary held Wood for one year before he made his third and final break from the Nashville stockade on February 16, 1921.[51] Much like his first bolt from the Tennessee Pen, no contemporary accounts surface on how Wood managed to escape, and Wood's memory of the event was cryptic at best. "I got all upset and escaped again," Wood lamented in his *Life History*. Despite the mystery surrounding his means of exiting the prison walls, Wood saw fit to give details on how he headed south to Winston-Salem, North Carolina. There he hoped to meet his wife, almost certainly Rushey (Hayes) Wood, and their young child, born in early 1919, around the time of Wood's escape from the West Virginia Penitentiary. Otto remembered that he ultimately planned to relocate his family to somewhere in the West.[52] Whether a part of his plans to gather funds for the move westward or part of no grand plan whatsoever, Wood began trafficking liquor in western North Carolina within a month of his flight from the Tennessee Penitentiary.

On the night of March 12, 1921, Wood flagged down a Buick jitney driven by Jack Cowan, a young man finishing his route running passengers between Statesville and Winston-Salem for his father's cab company. Otto convinced Cowan that he was seeking help for a carload of friends broken down on the highway closer to Winston-Salem. Wood hired Cowan to drive him north, instructing him to fill up his car at a gas station, remarking that their trip could extend farther than expected. On Wood's instruction, Cowan drove to the edge of a forested area located by the roadside past Mocksville. Wood exited the car briefly, then returned after searching for his own car out in the woods. For some unknown reason, Wood decided he should tell Cowan the truth: the carload of "five other people" was actually a load of whiskey. "[Wood] was surprised not to find the car," reported the *Statesville Landmark*, "and returned saying the liquor was there but he supposed the negro [an accomplice left to guard the car] had taken the car to a friend's [home] nearby."[53] Wood and Cowan continued their drive toward Winston-Salem. Reaching the city limits around three in the morning, Wood indicated that he thought something was wrong with the car and asked Cowan to get out to and check for a broken spring. Cowan returned to the cab to find that Wood had moved over to the driver's seat and was armed with a pistol. After checking Cowan to see that the young man was not carrying any weapons, Wood drove away.[54]

Jack Cowan immediately walked to the Winston-Salem police station and reported the stolen car. The young man identified Wood from a lineup of photographs of criminals known to operate in North Carolina.[55] The search for Wood, and for Cowan's car, continued for several months, resulting in one false arrest in Greenville, South Carolina—probably due to a man having one of the same physical handicaps as Wood.[56] Cowan's Buick reappeared in late April in a garage in Illinois, reportedly "damaged by wear and rough treatment." Wood, traveling with his wife and child, drove west before breaking down in Illinois. A towing company hauled the car to a nearby town, but locked Cowan's Buick in a garage when Wood refused to pay the $100 repair bill. Wood later broke into the garage and stole $200 worth of tires and another Buick. Looking for an artful way to say the thief was still on the lam, one Statesville, North Carolina, reporter stated that after Wood exited the Illinois garage, he promptly "lost himself again."[57]

Although vanished from the columns of North Carolina newshawks, Wood was far from dormant in his criminal activities in the summer and fall of 1921. Driving west with his wife and child, Otto reemerged a few months later in Texas under the alias "Jennings."[58] On the night of August 30, a bandit described as missing his left hand held up the car of C. A. Jettson and Annie Taylor on the road near Junction City, Texas. Wood robbed the couple, then forced them at gunpoint to drive him 150 miles to San Antonio.[59] The following evening, just outside the city, Wood attempted to hold up a car driven by T. J. O'Malley. When O'Malley tried to drive away during the holdup, Wood panicked and shot into the car. He wounded O'Malley and caused the car to wreck, injuring several of the passengers inside.[60]

Sending an alert to all police within two hundred miles of San Antonio, detectives tried to corner Wood multiple times. Despite failing to capture Otto, the lawmen succeeded in catching his wife and child and questioned them at the San Antonio Police Station concerning Wood's whereabouts. "There is no charges against her [Wood's wife] and she is free to come and go," stated one Texas reporter. "Her home is in Coledale [Coaldale], W. Va."[61] While his wife and child stayed with police in San Antonio, Wood stole another car and fled southwest toward the Mexican border. A garage owner from Eagle Pass, Texas, reported that "a stranger minus fingers on his left hand and shabbily dressed drove a dusty Dodge car to the Dixie Garage Friday afternoon [September 2]" and bought gasoline before driving to the border.[62]

In his *Life History* Wood remembered his time in Texas, claiming that he was a complete gentleman during the holdup of the couple outside of Junction City and altogether omitting his shooting of T. J. O'Malley. His account also featured a car chase, tangles with Mexican bandits, and a three-day marathon run from the Texas Rangers through "the burning sands" of the desert outside Sonora, Texas. After discovering that his wife and child had headed back east, Wood described traveling to the home of his mother, who had moved to Coaldale, West Virginia. Meeting his wife and child in Coaldale, Wood once again made plans to haul liquor, heading north toward the Ohio River to procure a car for that purpose.[63]

On September 23, Wood stole a Buick—by this point, his favorite make of car—in Portsmouth, Ohio, and drove south, intending to recross the Ohio River at Ironton, but officers captured Wood and carried him to jail in Portsmouth.[64] Wood pleaded "not guilty" to the charge of car theft in municipal court, making the feeble argument that he only intended to use the car to get to Ironton.[65] Booked under an alias, this time the fairly nondescript "Charles Jones," Wood caused a scene when he picked the lock of his cell and the door leading to the jail's corridor. He then fashioned a piece of steel, ripped from an old park bench repurposed for use by prisoners, to spring open the lock on the door leading to the jail's basement. Hearing the noise and finding the damaged basement door, the officer on duty removed his shoes and crept down the basement stairs, gun in hand. The officer reported finding Wood engaged in trying to pry the lock off the basement door to the outside of the jail. Moving Wood away from the door at gunpoint, the guard escorted the unsuccessful escape artist back upstairs to a different cell.[66]

After over a month's stay in the Portsmouth jail, Ohio authorities sent Wood, as "Charles Jones, 24, of Coaldale, W. Va.," to the Ohio State Penitentiary at Columbus.[67] Wood entered the penitentiary in mid-November 1921 and remained behind bars for nearly two years. In his *Life History*, Wood wrote that he was granted parole in June 1923.[68] Contradicting Wood's memory, the prison rolls state that he escaped from a road gang on June 21, 1923.[69]

Once again free from prison walls, Wood wasted little time in resuming his career as a highwayman. Assuming the name "Jack Boggs," Otto began haunting the roads of central Kentucky and Tennessee. On the night of September 14, 1923, a mile north of Bowling Green, Kentucky, Wood waylaid the car of Edgar Clemmons, a local department store clerk. Wood stood in the road displaying a pistol and called for Clemmons to stop his car. Clemmons immediately skidded to halt and fled from the car. Clemmons's run was cut short by Wood, who managed to catch him after a short distance and beat Clemmons over the head with a pistol. As Wood ordered Clemmons to hand over a pocket watch and some change—as well as his shirt, collar, and tie— a car driven by another local man, John Harris, pulled to a stop. Leveling his weapon into Harris's face, Wood ordered Harris to drive away. Harris drove straight to the Bowling Green Police Station to report the robbery.[70]

Police from Bowling Green, reporting to the scene of the crime later that evening, discovered a Studebaker stranded on the roadside a short distance away. They approached to find the car occupied by a woman and a one-year-old child. Giving her name as Mrs. Lucy Boggs of Cincinnati, Ohio, the woman admitted that her husband, Jack Boggs, also known as "Charles Woods," was the one who had assaulted and robbed Clemmons. Mrs. Boggs informed police that their car had run out of gas during a long trip from Nashville, Tennessee, and her husband had left the car, telling her he would walk to Bowling Green to get more gasoline. He had walked only a short distance from the car before bushwhacking Clemmons and disappearing into the night.[71] "Lucy Boggs," though perhaps a real name, was more likely an alias for one of the North Carolina women already confirmed to have connections with Wood.[72]

Five hours after robbing Clemmons, Wood broke into the Park City Motor Company's garage in Bowling Green. Holding night watchman Robert Rather hostage, Wood emptied the garage's cash drawers and selected a new Buick roadster to make his escape.[73] Wood then forced Rather into the Buick at gunpoint and ordered him to drive south toward Nashville, Tennessee. Reaching Nashville around dawn the next day, Wood ordered Rather from the car and drove away. Nashville police, following Rather's lead, tracked the car to a nearby depot, where they confirmed that a man matching Wood's description had bought a ticket on the train headed toward Louisville.[74]

Kentucky lawmen lost Wood's trail shortly thereafter and seem to have held Lucy Boggs and her child for only a brief period before releasing them.[75] One newspaper in Owensboro, Kentucky, tried to connect Wood with the killing of Patrolman Oglesby Dailey of Louisville, shot through the heart while engaged in a shootout with a burglar on the evening of September 12.[76] This slaying of a police officer was never fully connected with Otto Wood and seems largely out of character for Wood's crimes up to this point. Wood's modus operandi appears to have largely consisted of employing a firearm as a prop for intimidation, only using his pistol to bludgeon his victims when they seemed reticent to give him whatever he wanted to steal from them. The latter method of intimidation would, quite literally, result in a misfire for Wood in a Greensboro pawnshop several months later. This use of brute force would garner Wood a reputation as murderer and desperado, drawing wider attention from lawmen and the press in his home state of North Carolina.

CHAPTER 4

KILLING A RATTLESNAKE

THE GREENSBORO KILLING AND
THE 1924 PRISON ESCAPE, 1923–1924

Killing a rattlesnake does not stop other and alive snakes from bit-
ing people; but get this straight: it does everylastingly [*sic*] make
it impossible for the snake that has been killed to bite any more
people! In killing the snake you have not removed the menace of
snakes, as there are a lot of snakes left; but you have forever removed
any menace from that particular snake. Think it over.
—Billy Dock, Richmond, Virginia, to the *Statesville Record and
Landmark*, May 17, 1924, in "Otto Wood and Capital Punishment"

All of the "wild west" stuff isn't done for the movies. What director
could have staged anything more forceful than did Otto Wood in
his daring escape from the penitentiary. . . . It was a thriller through
and through even to the story told by Wood after the Roanoke police
had him in custody. Otto Wood is nobody's fool; and what a pity
the genius he displays in wrong doing could not have been better
directed. He is not all bad. . . . He has something of the gallantry of
the old-time bandit.
—"Page the Universal!," *Lexington Dispatch*, May 12, 1924

If Otto Wood serves out his sentence, 30 years, he will be 58 years
old. Why doesn't a person stop and think of the consequences before committing a crime?
—*North Wilkesboro Hustler*, January 17, 1924

He walked in a pawnshop, a rainy day, and with the clerk he
    had quarrel, they say,
He pulled out his gun and struck him a blow, this is the way
    the story goes . . .
—"Otto Wood the Bandit" by the Carolina Buddies, Columbia
    151345-2, recorded February 24, 1931, New York, New York

H. K. DEVERE STARED INTO the dim light of a jail cell. "Pick him out," ordered the voice of Guilford County sheriff D. B. Stafford. DeVere shifted his gaze through the swarm of faces that peered back from the cell until he settled on one. "That is the man," DeVere pointed, then looked straight into the eyes of the prisoner, who, even after DeVere's affirmation, showed no sign of recognition or nervousness. Despite the collected appearance of the man behind the bars, DeVere knew that this was the face of the gunman who had jumped into his car and forced him to speed out of Greensboro, North Carolina, on the morning of November 3, 1923. Determined to call the detached con's bluff, the witness repeated his accusation in the form of a statement: "We are meeting under different circumstances." As DeVere spoke these words, the prisoner dropped his eyes. That motion did not escape the notice of Sheriff Stafford, who watched as the convict slowly turned pale. His suspicions revealed, Stafford reported to the press that the city of Greensboro had its man, the outlaw Otto Wood.[1]

In the fall of 1923, Wilkes County's most notorious son once again brought trouble home to North Carolina when a deadly exchange of blows with pawnbroker Abraham Wolf Kaplan of Greensboro marked him as a murderer. Kaplan, a Jewish Russian immigrant, had made his home in the southern city and ran a pawnshop in the downtown district.[2] Wood entered Kaplan's shop on the morning of November 3, supposedly to reclaim a pawned pocket watch.[3] As Wood later recounted, an argument ensued that escalated until Kaplan raised a stick to strike him. In an attempt to defend himself, Wood pistol-whipped Kaplan over the head, a blow that caused the pistol to misfire, discharging a round into the pawnbroker's shoulder. Wood later downplayed the wounds he gave Kaplan in a 1925 interview. "I didn't kill that man," he demurred. "The doctors operated and he never came out from under the ether. He didn't have anything but a little scalp wound and I know that didn't kill him."[4] This "scalp wound" was a fractured skull, which caused Kaplan's death.[5]

In his *Life History*, Wood underlined his claim that he possessed no knowledge of Kaplan's death until several weeks later in mid-November 1924. He recollected, "I had not before heard of his death and was very surprised for I had no idea of killing him."[6] Though newspapers offered only vague mention of the specific details that surrounded Kaplan's last hours, some accounts, such as one relayed to the *Washington Post*, disclosed the ultimate cause of death as "injuries received when [Kaplan] was attacked in his shop."[7] The *Statesville Landmark* later divulged that Kaplan "on his death bed" said "he was beaten and shot by a man with only one arm."[8] It seems clear, based on Wood's previous activities during this time period, that he was intent on robbing Kaplan from the time he entered the pawnbroker's shop. The clubbing of Kaplan over the head with a pistol matches Wood's actions in the robbery of Edgar Clemmons a month earlier and adds some credence to Wood's story that firing into Kaplan's shoulder was accidental.[9]

Wood's escape from Greensboro involved an almost theatrical sense of timing and attracted the attention of Piedmont and western North Carolina newspapers for nearly a month. After he wounded Kaplan, Wood rushed from the pawnshop into the middle of South Elm Street, where he leaped onto a passing Gardner touring car and ordered driver H. K. DeVere to drive northwest and exit the city. In the countryside on the periphery of Greensboro, Wood forced DeVere out of the automobile, removed the driver's coat and hat, and demanded that DeVere "shell out" $150 from his pockets.[10] Officers on South Elm Street immediately arrested a man named "Allred" in the frenzy that followed the shooting, but released him after realizing he looked nothing like Kaplan's assailant. The car stolen by Wood reappeared in Greensboro "in the dead of night," a trick that caused headlines to marvel at his surreptitiousness in returning the automobile "as quietly as if he had been a ghost."[11] Before exiting Greensboro again on the evening of November 4, Wood held up John Allison, a local man walking near the tracks of the Atlantic and Yadkin Railroad. Perhaps not inclined to conduct another violent robbery after shooting Kaplan, the bandit simply asked Allison whether he had any money. After Allison responded that he had none on his person, Wood walked away toward the city's business district. Police later speculated that Wood walked back into town to catch a train to escape once again.[12]

As the Greensboro police investigated Kaplan's murder, the search for Wood's whereabouts escalated into a manhunt. Greensboro chief of police George Crutchfield left the city to search for Wood in the hills of Wilkes County only to find that Wood's mother had left the Dellaplane community for West Virginia, almost two years prior to his arrival. Guilford County and the city of Greensboro declared Wood an outlaw, and county commissioners levied twin rewards of $100 for his apprehension. An additional reward of $500 provided by Kaplan's widow quickly raised even more attention for the fugitive, making Wood an outlaw for the second time in his life.[13] The price on Wood's head eventually climbed to a grand total of $1,200.[14]

Kentucky newspapers quickly picked up the story, acknowledging Wood as the same highwayman who had operated around Bowling Green only two months earlier.[15] The manhunt also attracted the attention of the Department of Justice: an Agent Meekins, headquartered in Charlotte, North Carolina, circulated Wood's picture and informed the press of Wood's previous crimes. Meekins recounted the details of Wood's car thefts in south Texas in 1921 and, while acknowledging some uncertainty, connected the outlaw with murder charges in Indiana and Illinois.[16] These latter charges appear to have had no connection to Wood and never reappeared in later narratives listing his crimes.

Wood evaded authorities until November 10, 1923, when lawmen cornered him in the vicinity of Bramwell in Mercer County, West Virginia.[17] The posse discovered a hidden North Carolina license tag as well as a Ford coupe missing from the Davidson Motor Company of Lexington, North Carolina, parked near the home of Wood's relatives, later revealed as either the home of Ellen Wood or that of Henry Pardue, Wood's brother-in-law, in the community of Freeman, West Virginia.[18] After the officers arrested him, Wood gave reporters trivial misleading and false details: for example, that police had located the car in Pocahontas, in neighboring Tazewell County, Virginia, and not in Mercer County, West Virginia.[19] The West Virginia officers held Wood in the jail at Princeton until the arrival of Chief of Police Crutchfield from Greensboro on November 14.[20] No matter how much the snared fugitive argued his case, the coupling of the stolen car with the description given by Kaplan doomed any chance of his acquittal.

Bound and gagged after his capture, Wood created a stir among Greensboro's citizens on his return following an overnight train ride from southern West Virginia. "It looked like a funeral party," recalled one reporter, who watched the shackled bandit slowly walk to the jail surrounded by a "flock of policemen." To prevent Wood from making a break, the officers rigged a rope on his neck and fastened it into a knot around his arms so that any swift movement caused him to choke. A journalist from the *Greensboro Daily News*, among the first to encounter the infamous character, offered a biography as well as an up-close description of the bandit's features gleaned from a brief interview:

His name is Otto H. Wood, though he is sometimes called C. H. Wood. He is 27 years old and was born and lived his early life in Wilkes County. About 15 years ago he moved to West Virginia and has been living there since. He is a mechanic, he said, but has been working in mines in West Virginia. As to his past criminal record he would not talk except to deny that he had ever been a prisoner in the Tennessee penitentiary.

He spoke freely and answered all other questions. In appearance he is neat and clean looking, a decided blonde with big blue eyes that slightly protrude from his head. He has high and prominent cheek bones and they and his eyes are the most striking features of his face. He wore a blue suit, tap shoes, low white collar and soft hat.

The left arm and hand which have been the subject of much discussion he kept partly hidden. The arm was in his trousers pocket and he held it there all the time he was talking. Unless looking for it, you would probably not have noticed that he has no left hand.[21]

The description of a dapper, well-dressed, free-speaking man struck much contrast with Wood's outlaw persona. Instead of a roughneck, the personality who greeted reporters and witnesses in his cell emanated a level-headed and sophisticated quality. The disparity in image even caused one witness to deny his certainty that the person behind the bars resembled the individual who sported "old clothes and a growth of beard" outside Kaplan's pawnshop on November 3.[22]

The "Jekyll and Hyde" aspect of Wood's character became further accentuated as witnesses shuffled through the Greensboro cell block. W. R. Melvin, a night watchman at a local garage, identified Wood as the robber who accosted him on the night of July 12, 1923, and then coerced him to drive to Winston-Salem, placing Wood in North Carolina shortly before his Kentucky crime spree. The stolen car Wood used to travel to Winston before leaving Melvin later reemerged in Radford, Virginia, abandoned in alley.[23] Hearing Melvin's story, Chief of Police Crutchfield further speculated that Wood was responsible for the robbery of Mr. and Mrs. John T. Rees, accosted by a highwayman in Greensboro at around the same time. Crutchfield also vaguely attached Wood to break-ins at the homes of several prominent Greensboro residents, including that of insurance magnate Julian Price, in the weeks preceding Kaplan's murder.[24] All speculations made by Crutchfield aside, the witness testimonies from several parties confirmed that Wood was no stranger to Greensboro. The narratives surrounding the highway robberies of Melvin and the Reeses match Wood's known manner of procuring cars and money, more than likely connected to his continued hauling of bootleg liquor from Wilkes into the urban areas of the Piedmont.

Despite descriptions of crimes that painted him as an all-around hoodlum and highwayman, Wood's charm from behind prison bars convinced officials and the public that they dealt not with a desperate murderer but with a thief whose botched robbery accidently caused the death of a local businessman. From inside his cell, Wood continued to deny his involvement in the murder of Kaplan and insisted that he could produce ten to fifteen "good people . . . not members of [his] family" with "no connection" who could verify his presence in West Virginia on November 3. With a show of confidence, Wood boasted to reporters that he "was not afraid to face a jury."[25]

Whether an accident or a deliberate act of murder, the death of Kaplan resulted in a charge far more serious than any Wood had previously faced in North Carolina. In a narrative of the trial held in the Guilford County courthouse on December 24, one reporter remarked on Wood's serene demeanor as he received the verdict of second-degree murder with a thirty-year sentence of hard labor in the North Carolina State Prison.[26] The article mentioned his wife and child—without offering any names or further description—as seated next to him when the judge announced the sentence. A Mount Airy, North Carolina, newspaper placed the story underneath the bold subhead "Cool Killer Thinks Verdict About Right."[27] Wood expressed his feelings about the trial to reporters shortly after his sentencing: "Maybe if my record had not been against me I might have got manslaughter. But the verdict is just about what I expected. . . . I'm going to try and show the people of North Carolina that I can be a decent man and if they think so they can give me another chance. But if they don't think so I'll serve the whole time."[28] The report also identified Wood as an already notable character to North Carolinians, calling Wood "the most hard-boiled proposition that has come into the criminal limelight this year. . . . Like a slippery eel he usually got away with his rascality." The *Mt. Airy News* spoke for local sentiment around the community of Jonesville, some twenty miles east of North Wilkesboro, where residents readily acknowledged their neighbor Wood's known participation in car thefts and robberies.[29]

The trial and the details of the crime prominently occupied the front page of newspapers around Wood's home in Wilkes County. The *Wilkes Journal-Patriot* remarked that the young man received the verdict "with the coolness that has been the marvel of the oldest courtroom habitué" and appeared markedly relieved by the fact he did not receive a more severe sentence.[30] The Wilkes reporter devoted the bulk of the column to reprinting a transcript of an extensive speech given by Judge Thomas J. Shaw. Shaw's speech embodied much of the public opinion formed around Wood during his stay in the Greensboro jail. Speaking with "deep feeling" toward Wood, Shaw explained the comparative lightness of Wood's sentence:

> Mr. Wood, the jury returned a verdict of murder in the second degree. As I stated yesterday, I approve of that verdict. The truth is that on Saturday before the solicitor addressed the jury I told him that it was a case of murder in the second degree and that if the jury returned a verdict of murder in the first degree I would set it aside.

I think it is much better to have a verdict in the second degree, though, than for it to have been ordered by the court, but even if it is only the crime of murder in the second degree it is a very very serious crime.

It is not necessary for me to talk to you. A man of as much good common sense as you have that will quit work to go out and steal and kill, there is really very little excuse for him. Now if a man has an unbalanced mind, if his mentality is deficient and he goes out and commits a crime there is not any excuse for it. But there is more excuse than for a person who has good common sense as you have.

It is written in the Bible, "Be sure your sins will find you out." The mills of justice grind slowly sometimes, but they grind; and if people would only think about that, when they commit a crime and escape the probabilities are that they will be caught and punished for it, I do not think there would be nearly so many crimes committed.[31]

The sermon-like quality of Shaw's verdict hinted that the state of North Carolina, as early as 1923, had decided to make a public example of Wood. The suave appearance he maintained while in the Greensboro jail, coupled with his apparent practicality and display of common sense, made him a character, though disreputable, both sympathetic and altogether vivid in the public conscience of the Tar Heel State. Wood donned the guise of a symbolic man of the people, a victim whose situation in life led him blindly off the path of an increasingly progressive South. The attention of the public eye during the Greensboro trial was not lost on Wood. As evidenced by his letters to the *Wilkes Journal-Patriot* in 1917, Wood already understood the power of the press. Acknowledging Wood's use of the press to shape his own persona throughout the 1920s, a Raleigh, North Carolina, columnist later remarked: "[Wood] always liked publicity and staged his crimes in public places to attract attention."[32] The events in the months that followed only added to Wood's celebrity and gradually began to solidify his reputation as a calculating, resourceful, and often outspoken fugitive.

On the morning of May 10, 1924, little more than five months after his trial, Wood once again made headlines when he broke out of the North Carolina penitentiary in Raleigh, alongside fellow convict, J. H. Starnes, a Forsyth County man sentenced to five years for larceny.[33] Wood's escape began in the prison supply room, where he grabbed chair factory overseer L. A. Partin around the neck. Starnes and another inmate, Sidney Gupton, threatened to kill Partin with cane knives if he shouted the alarm. With the overseer's pistol in hand, Wood then requisitioned the automobile of prison physician Dr. J. N. Norman and, with the gun pressed against Partin's ribs, forced him

Otto Wood, ca. 1923, around the time of his incarceration
in the North Carolina State Prison. Image from *Life
History of Otto Wood*. (Author's collection)

to make a calm show as he drove Starnes and Wood past an unsuspecting
guard and out through the prison gates. The runaways drove into Raleigh's
Seaboard Air Line railyards, where they strong-armed Partin from the car.[34]
Driving through the Capitol district pursued by prison guards and Raleigh
police, Wood and Starnes paused briefly along New Bern Avenue to abandon
Norman's car and climb onto a bakery truck driven by M. V. Sanderford.
Forcing Sanderford at gunpoint to drive them out of town, the fugitives rode
toward Durham, still wearing their blue prison overalls. That afternoon, the
escaped convicts left Sanderford and the truck about ten miles from the
Durham city limits.[35]

In the early morning hours of Sunday, May 11, the duo jumped onto the
running boards of a Studebaker driven by M. D. Cline, a Durham native
returning home from a weekend fishing trip. Starnes held a pistol on Cline

through the window from his perch on the left running board, demanding that Cline surrender the wheel as Wood slid into the car. Wood drove slowly toward Greensboro on rain-slicked roads while Starnes steadied his revolver on Cline from the back seat, bragging that "they had just escaped from the State's prison." Wood flicked a match so Cline could see a news clipping: "See there. That's my picture."[36] As Starnes continued to cover Cline, making sure he would not cry out for help, Wood drove through Greensboro at around six in the morning.[37] In a woodland area just outside the city, the escapees ordered Cline out of the car and proceeded to drag him toward a barbed wire fence located about two hundred yards from the road. When Cline tried to struggle, Starnes clobbered him over the head with his pistol. Wood and Starnes then bound Cline's hands, gagged him with a handkerchief, and used his belt to tie him to the fence. After they removed $30 and a watch from Cline's pockets, Wood and Starnes walked back toward the car. One of the duo shot their gun in the air "five or six times in rapid succession" with what Cline remembered as a "bravado" that seemed the pantomime of a "Wild West thriller."[38] Cline's testimony only added to the folklore that had already formed around Wood's exploits and further solidified his image as something akin to film depictions of an Old West desperado.

W. J. Ladd, a night watchman at local filling station, confirmed that Wood and Starnes stopped and ordered him to fill their car with gas before leaving Greensboro that evening. Ladd claimed that he identified Otto as the duo drove away. "I noticed the ears and knew it was Otto," Ladd told reporters. "I could tell from his pictures I've seen in the newspapers." When asked why he did not attempt to stop Wood, Ladd shrugged. "Yes and why didn't I? Just why didn't I?" Ladd repeated. Acknowledging Wood and Starnes were armed, a reporter for the *Statesville Landmark* kidded that "[Ladd] knew exactly why he didn't [make an attempt to stop Wood]."[39]

From Greensboro, the fugitives made their way west to Winston-Salem, where they picked up Wood's wife and daughter—by some accounts forcing them to come along at gunpoint—then continued their journey over the Virginia line. Before they crossed into Henry County, Virginia, Wood and Starnes drove on country lanes to bypass the more populated sections of Martinsville, to the south, and Rocky Mount, to the north in Franklin County. Traffic policemen later reported that they had tried to flag down a speeding Studebaker in the locality of Schoolfield, just south of Danville, before the car "headed for open country" south of the North Carolina line.[40] At around 2 a.m. on May 12, Henry County officers searching for the escaped convicts inadvertently captured two cars carrying a combined 222 gallons of moonshine liquor. The blockaders, later identified as Henry County locals, fled on foot after stopping short of the officers' cars, parked as a makeshift roadblock.[41]

On the afternoon of May 12, 1924, a Roanoke, Virginia, police officer noticed a mud- splattered car with an obscured license plate idling on a street in the heart of the "Magic City."[42] The car lingered in front of the home of J. H. Starnes's wife on Centre Avenue. With Wood and his family waiting in the car, Starnes met his wife on the porch, intending to convince her to come with him on the run. Starnes bolted from the porch when two policemen on motorcycles began riding toward the car, jumping in as Wood hammered on the gas pedal.[43] The officers trailed the car to a nearby field, where Wood and Starnes fled from the vehicle—leaving Wood's wife and child—and "darted off" into a nearby section of woods. Railroad detectives and Roanoke police combed the city, tracking the fugitives to a Norfolk and Western railyard on the city's west side. By six that evening, eleven officers, three private detectives, and a posse of hastily recruited railroad employees surrounded the two escaped prisoners in the railyard. Having only one .25 caliber automatic revolver between them, Wood and Starnes realized they had no chance against the posse and peacefully surrendered.[44] "No doubt exhaustion had much to do with the tameness of the end of the hunt," wrote one Greensboro columnist.[45] The Roanoke officers split the $700 reward for the capture and return of the prisoners, levied during their two-day run.[46]

Covering the aftermath of the manhunt, a Virginia reporter relayed the conversation between Roanoke's Chief of Police Taylor and Mrs. Wood, taken into custody along with her daughter. The geography given in this interview all but confirms Rushey (Hayes) Wood as the identity of the wife interviewed by Taylor. Rushey Wood told Taylor the details of how she and her daughter were compelled to accompany Otto Wood and Starnes:

> Mrs. Wood told the police that she was boarding with one sister in Winston-Salem and had been visiting with another sister when the auto containing her husband and Starnes drove up in front of her door. . . . They had inquired at the home of the sister where Mrs. Wood made her home and were told where she was visiting and without fear they drove to that place. . . . Wood entered the house and told his wife they had no time to lose and that she and the child should join him in the stolen automobile. Mrs. Wood told Major Taylor that she refused to go, whereupon her husband threatened her with death. Then she relented and with her child she boarded the automobile . . . [with Otto driving the car]. She sat on the front seat with her daughter, she said, and Starnes occupied the rear seat alone.[47]

Rushey's description of the trip to Roanoke recounted a grueling drive on back roads: the car sometimes sank up to the tires in mud from recent heavy rains.[48] A later interview confirms that Rushey was in the process of seeking a divorce from Wood during this period, having begun to distance herself from Otto shortly after his sentencing to the North Carolina State Prison. This interview adds credence to the story that Wood forced her and their daughter to join him and Starnes on the journey toward Roanoke.[49]

The sensational stories that surrounded the prison break solidified Wood's persona as a tactful, admirable fugitive with a well-timed sense of wit. On his return to prison after a two-day flight into southern Virginia, one reporter commented: "Wood makes it hard to hold what is unquestionably the right opinion about his activities. He is a bad egg, a dangerous man but somehow his engaging candor disarms criticism and takes all the pleasure out of news of his capture."[50] "I told Warden Busbee," Wood remarked to the press, "that if I did not get a square deal I would be compelled to leave. [Warden Busbee] replied that if it was easy as that to go ahead." One article described the highlight of the escape as the fugitives' return of the prison physician's car. The journalist painted the scene in broad comedic strokes and related how Wood "disliked the idea of putting the doctor to any unnecessary trouble, so he decided to leave the car where its owner would surely find it . . . the heart of the city of Raleigh . . . Capitol Square."[51]

Another reporter, not nearly as enthralled by Wood's antics, took a more critical stance on North Carolina's number one trickster: "Professional reformers will hardly get excited at the wild statements made by Otto Wood and his partner . . . charging brutal treatment and improper care at the state prison. Neither of these gentlemen might be called impartial witnesses. . . . It is an old trick for fellows like Wood to issue statements. He covets the limelight and it is written of him that he took great delight in reading the thrilling stories he furnished the papers by his daring escape."[52] Despite such sentiments, journalists throughout the Old North State recognized the potential gold mine of a twentieth-century "Jesse James." "Fiction pales in comparison to the truth concerning the amazing exploits in which Wood now figures," wrote one enthusiastic newsman.[53] Aside from his killing of Kaplan, the reports about Wood highlighted his relative lack of ruthlessness as he dodged across the countryside pursued by posses and scores of lawmen. The outlaw made for steady front-page readership, and subscribers eagerly consumed articles to discover more about the personality of the state's favorite criminal.

Wood's celebrity caused a flurry of newspaper activity concerning not only his actions but also the effectiveness of North Carolina's prison system and

the general welfare of the state. The much-debated issue of capital punishment emerged as a leading argument within articles and editorials responding to those members of the public who found the criminal's antics amus-
ing. "The Charlotte Observer thinks that the menace of a fellow like Otto
Wood . . . is sufficient to answer to those who would abolish capital punishment," opined one North Carolina editor, "but the anti–capital punishment
advocates center all their interest and sympathy on criminals. They are so
taken up with the criminals that they never give a thought to the victims."[54]
In another article, a more jovial columnist offered a tongue-in-cheek suggestion that the state use Otto Wood as a form of traffic control. "If Wood and
a few of his kind could be turned loose on the highways with instructions
to hold up only those who violate traffic laws," the journalist quipped, "the
speed fiends and road hogs would quickly change their ways."[55] The various
social topics attached to Wood's name ranged across and encapsulated the
troubles of a state struggling to understand itself and its people as it ad-
justed to the modernity of the Roaring Twenties. The policing of new roads
and a prison population on the rise offered just two key problems, seen as
side effects of uneven economic growth and societal stresses that troubled
politicians and private citizens alike.

Throughout the spring and summer of 1924, Wood added his own voice
to the debates surrounding his persona. The outlaw's written opinions en-
compassed both moral and social talking points as well as his own personal
troubles behind prison walls. The statements issued by Wood to the press
dovetailed perfectly with the ongoing arguments of newsprint commentators. In the few short lines he composed in letters to newspaper readers, the
infamous jailbird outlined the reasons behind his escape: "It is the harsh
treatment that a poor devil gets that turns him against the public and society and the inhuman treatment."[56] In another post, the convict complained
that his daily meals consisted only of "six salty crackers and a glass of water."
Wood further related that after "three negro prisoners brought him water in
a talcum powder can to relieve his thirst," the warden ordered them moved
to another part of the penitentiary. "I am slipping this out," whispered the
prisoner's pen, "and pray that whoever gets this letter will investigate at
once."[57] With these letters, Wood shifted the blame for his crimes from
himself to the society that built him—one that had failed to notice those
mired in poverty and neglect amid an era of supposed progress.

Further newspaper coverage complicated Wood's plea and challenged
the validity of his claims of harsh treatment by prison officials. The *Statesville Landmark*, in an article relayed from Raleigh, published the account of
Greensboro lawyer Allen Adams, who visited Wood in his cell on August 14.

Instead of the dire conditions described in the bandit's letter to the press, Adams found Wood in a "sufficiently lighted and ventilated cell" where the inmate read and reclined on a "cot as good as the officers and the men of our army had for use in the best canonments [sic]." The lawyer commented on the decorated walls of the cell, graced by numerous images of "feminine pulchritude," and described the scene as resembling that of "the average college freshman's domicile" instead of the cell of a "person who has been constitutionally convicted of taking unlawfully the life of a fellow human being." Prison officials allowed Adams to offer Wood cigarettes and carry on a brief conversation during which Adams tried to discover the truth of the prisoner's situation. "I asked how he was getting along," Adams reported, "[Wood] replied that he had no complaint to make other than that Superintendent Pou would not let him go back to the chair factory from which he made his celebrated escape some three months ago." After Adams read Wood's plea in a regional newspaper, the lawyer remarked that he "felt it [was his] duty to say something" due to the "gross inaccuracies and glaring mis-statements in Otto Wood's letter."[58]

Reporters further used these glaring inaccuracies to cast Wood as a pampered convict with unrealistic expectations of prison life. "Not a Health Resort," read a response to one of Wood's letters to the press. "Wood ought to remember that the State prison is not a health resort catering to the well disposed and fat pursed," remarked the columnist, "[but] rather a home for incurables like himself." Though he acknowledged there were "things wrong with the prison," the columnist admonished readers not to "fret over conditions as reported by this Wood." Despite this critical tone, the author took time to express personal sentiment about the treatment of prisoners and recommended that the prison system should focus more on humane conditions in order to rehabilitate its inmates. In one final admonition, the writer expressed hope that "no one will rave over the general subject of prison reform because of Otto Wood."[59] Rather than suppressing any explosion of commentary, the article elicited more opinions. As one Richmond, Virginia, reader expressed his thoughts to the editor of the *Statesville Landmark*: "That perfect saint, the aforesaid Otto Wood, has got the cart before the horse: It's the inhuman treatment that society gets at the hands of the criminal that causes society to restrain him. Society—and I use the word 'society' to indicate law-abiding people—does not raise its hand against the individual until the individual has raised his hand against law and order. Otto Wood was at liberty to do as he pleased as long as what he pleased to do was not a transgression of the rights of other people."[60] The article also compared Wood and other criminals to "rattlesnakes," making the case that "all criminals"—apparently not even just those convicted of murder—should suffer execution. "I can see no reason whatever for temporizing with an animal [meaning any criminal] that is a menace to society," the declared the Virginia writer.[61] The harshness of the Virginia writer's stance reveals one extreme opinion of criminals during the era.

Despite the number of naysayers who confronted Wood's push to become a hero, standing up for the rights of his fellow prisoners, his image as a people's champion against a corrupt society gradually began to surface as newspapers printed more columns about his adventures both outside and inside prison walls. Wood enjoyed reading about his own exploits, and his neighbors throughout North Carolina and the greater Southeast soon became equally indulgent. Publications such as the *Lexington Dispatch* suggested that the public disregard Wood—a sentiment reflecting knowledge of how intently the public already read and listened to Wood's opinions. The spectacle produced by the 1924 escape, portrayed as an exercise in crime with conscience, completely lampooned the state of North Carolina and its prison system. As the stories of his experiences flooded the press, the legendary phenomenon behind "Otto Wood the Robin Hood" received all the dry kindling needed to burst into a wildfire.

CHAPTER 5

THE HOUDINI OF CELL BLOCK A

OTTO WOOD, CRIMINAL CELEBRITY,

1925–1928

In the files at the State Prison there is a record of this man, who has been called the "Houdini of cell block A" because of his habit of vanishing under the very guns of prison guards . . .
—"State Prison Houdini," *Asheville (NC) Citizen-Times*,
   September 7, 1930

Fellow convicts called him "Houdini" Wood but prison officials call him plain lucky. . . . Desperate though he is, Wood, according to prison authorities, used to receive considerable "fan" mail from feminine admirers.
—"One Armed Convict Escapes," *Hope (AR) Star*, July 19, 1930

When it comes to personality, Otto Wood is vivid. . . . No more need be said for his versatility than to point out the loss of one arm was no more handicap to his attending to the wheel and the maiden than to his keeping a victim covered with his pistol hand, while he relieved him of his wallet. . . . Otto has given the word "ambidextrous" a new and mysterious definition.
—*Statesville (NC) Record and Landmark*, November 15, 1926

He was known throughout the land
For he had one only hand
But in bravery journeyed on his merry way . . .
—"Otto Wood," recorded by Cranford and Thompson,
   Champion 17486, January 27, 1931, Richmond, Indiana

WHY DIDN'T YOU LEAVE North Carolina and stay gone when you had a chance?" The question rose from within the crowd of reporters and onlookers gathered inside the Iredell County jail on December 7, 1925. Throughout the day, hundreds of Carolinians, described as ranging from "banker to bum," visited the cell of "North Carolina's craftiest convict." The impromptu open house offered an up-close view of Otto Wood, who greeted reporters and spectators alike from the comfort of his cell. "Oh, I like North Carolina: it's a good state, besides all my people live here," Wood explained to one reporter. "The real reason I didn't light out for West Virginia was on account of my mother. She asked me to come back and give up. . . . It's my babies and my mother that gets me worried."[1]

Two weeks had passed since Wood's second break from the North Carolina State Prison in Raleigh on November 23. As in his second escape from the Tennessee Penitentiary in 1917, Wood rode out of the prison grounds in a railcar. "I had clothes under my prison clothes," Wood told the press, "so when I got a chance I got into the boxcar where I had been loading tile . . . just took off my prison clothes and rode out."[2] Other accounts explained that Wood's escape was not nearly as simple as he outlined to reporters. Wood took advantage of smoke from a burning barn on the nearby campus of the North Carolina School for the Blind. Using the smoke to screen his entrance into the boxcar, Wood climbed into one of the culvert pipes stacked inside.[3] The escape artist was also carrying a stolen sledgehammer and used it to break through the locked door after the car stopped in the railyard beyond the prison walls. Wood quickly exchanged his prison clothes for a khaki overcoat and a stolen pair of "citizen's pants"—nonstriped pants issued to honor prisoners.[4] The fugitive then proceeded to walk through downtown Raleigh, passing by several people who later admitted noticing his distinctive limp but having no idea he was an escaped prisoner.[5] At nine o'clock that night, realizing Wood had managed to escape again, prison superintendent George Ross Pou levied a reward of $50 for Wood's capture. Pou's reward was immediately bolstered with an additional $250 from Governor Angus McLean.[6]

Leaving Raleigh, Wood traveled via freight train to Florence, Alabama, and from there caught a train to Winston-Salem, North Carolina. Wood then traveled north, either by train or stolen car, to visit his relatives in the coalfields of West Virginia.[7] The following week, in Stokes County, North Carolina, residents reported a man matching Wood's description trying to hitchhike to Martinsville.[8] Paralleling his travels after his 1917 escape from the Tennessee Penitentiary, Wood's extended tour culminated a week later, joyriding in a stolen car around his home community in Wilkes County. The *North Wilkesboro Hustler* announced Wood's return to Dellaplane:

> Monday's *Charlotte Observer* says "Otto Wood, escaped convict, blew into his old home community last night and spent today 'joy riding' over the Boone Trail, eight miles west of this city." . . . Wood was certainly in Wilkes county Saturday night . . . from the best information

obtainable from those who have known him from the days of his youth, and who have resided for years in the Dellaplane section of this county, where he was born, the escaped convict arrived at a late hour last night. From what part of the state he travelled is not known. He talked to several citizens of the Dellaplane section just after his arrival. . . . [Wood is] driving a Dodge sedan.[9]

The joy ride literally screeched to a halt on December 7 in neighboring Iredell County. Wood made the mistake of riding through Statesville's main street, where residents recognized him as he pulled up at a traffic stop. Police attempted to give chase but reportedly went the wrong direction, confused as to what route Wood used to speed out of town. Wood's luck ran out an hour later when Mooresville police chief Otis Woodsides stood in the middle of the highway and leveled a rifle at the windshield of Wood's car. The fugitive surrendered to Woodsides, who later described his captive as "very affable and agreeable."[10] Held in the Iredell County jail, Wood tried to convince reporters that he was traveling back to the state prison when captured.[11] After a brief stay in the Iredell County jail, where he talked with reporters and the public—who were somehow allowed to talk to Wood before being ushered from the cell block by Sheriff Woodsides—Wood returned to Raleigh. Prison officials placed Wood in solitary confinement in hopes of impeding the possibility of any further escapes. As Wood languished in his cell, one headline relayed the highlights of Wood's break in the same manner as a recurrent sporting event, nonchalantly dubbing his second break the "Annual Vacation of Otto Wood."[12]

In a twenty-two-month period from the fall of 1925 to the late summer months of 1927, the myth of "Otto Wood the Bandit" rapidly took shape. The larger-than-life persona of the Carolina desperado hinged on a series of escapes, beginning with the 1925 break, that elevated Wood to the status of a celebrity. Through letters to the press, posed as orations to the people of North Carolina, as well as a self-published autobiography, Wood took an active part in the mythmaking process. The escape artist and highwayman pitched his story in part by blaming the errors of his ways on his hard-scrabble roots. As Wood constructed his portrait, he held up a mirror to the face of society and further pleaded his case as a victim of a corrupt prison system. Wood's publication of his life story and frequent contact with the press yielded attention that bordered on mania as newspapers and the public both celebrated and criticized Wood's rebellion against authority.

Wood's December 1925 "vacation" produced much fervor among the press and led to published debates printed in the early months of 1926. Aware

of the press's power, Wood acknowledged his own indulgence in the stories told about him by reporters and joked about their presentation. "I read
the papers all the time. . . . [The *Greensboro News*] had a picture of me on
the front page. Didn't think much of the picture," he smiled with a "gold-
toothed" grin. "Ain't near as handsome as me." In a more serious tone,
Wood addressed charges of antisemitism and hostility toward the friends
of the pawnbroker Kaplan, whom Wood killed in Greensboro. "Some fellow
named Huffman in Raleigh told the *Greensboro News* that I was on my way
to Greensboro to get another Jew," Wood testified. "I never said any such
thing and would like for the people to know I didn't." As to allegations of
threats against the husband of his now ex-wife, Rushey Hayes Austin of
Winston-Salem, Wood once again denied any intimation of violence. As the
newspaper attention increased, Otto made sure to use all interviews to his
advantage, spinning his own story to the public.[13]

Among those averse to the limelight placed on Wood, North Carolina
governor Angus Wilton McLean berated the focus on the criminal celebrity
as "foolishness." "The fact that Wood succeeded in getting away without
getting killed does not prove he is a hero," the governor remarked.[14] Yet in
the same issue of the *Gastonia Daily Gazette* that held the governor's comments, another article featured a much more admirable description of the
famed bandit:

> Wood is not the common type of criminal and never has been a "bad
> man" in the sense which the public usually considers the term . . . a cold-
> blooded, "shootin', fightin', son-of-a-gun." . . . He said he never had shot
> anyone and that it was beneath his code of ethics to do so. . . . Had it not
> been for his prison garb, an outsider would never have pictured him as
> a slayer and a "bad man." He is above average mentally, has a pleasing
> sense of humor, and . . . can laugh heartily when he recalls some pleasing
> experience. . . . He has nothing that would denote subnormelity [*sic*].[15]

Responding to the fascination with Wood's escapes, McLean countered
Wood's "above average" image as he reiterated his belief in the security of
the state prison. He tactfully demeaned Wood's fame as an escape artist,
remarking that prison facilities "are not so perfect that they preclude the
possibility of escape if a man is willing to sell his life."[16]

Although faced with the bulwark of political opposition from North
Carolina's highest office, Wood circumvented any need to bargain with authorities by telling his story directly to the people. His most direct appeal
to the public arrived during the summer of 1926 in the form of a small,

self-published pamphlet titled *Life History of Otto Wood*. In thirty-four pages
an outwardly repentant Otto Wood presented his own narrative of his life
of crime and attempted to subvert the news stories that depicted him as
a murderer. Initial commentary on *Life History* proved lighthearted. One
reviewer lauded the book in tongue-in-cheek fashion and suggested that
with a more apt title the book "might have been called 'How I Got In and
Out Only to Get Back In.'"[17] "[Wood] regards North Carolina as a great state,"
kidded another columnist, "and declares that he would rather be in state's
prison in North Carolina than a fleeing criminal elsewhere. No Rotarion, no
Kiwanian, no nobody has ever said a finer thing about the state."[18]

Despite the stream of jokes, the precedent set by Wood's publication
proved unnerving to officials as the popular criminal continued building
his own public persona. "There is something out of keeping with orderly
thought for the state to be allowing a cheap criminal to be publishing and
selling such a book," argued a *Mount Airy News* reporter. "Mr. Wood should
be bottoming chairs or even doing nothing rather than flooding the State
with such literature as he can produce." The Mount Airy writer further alleged that "somebody outside of the prison is making money on this deal,"
theorizing that much of Wood's publicity stemmed from commercial back-
ing.[19] Another journalist seconded the potential profitability of Wood's
bandit image, acknowledging that "Mr. Wood has the mercantile instinct
developed. . . . The public will read the book."[20]

Wood himself entered the war of words about his pamphlet and expressed his intentions to deliver his story as a tale on morality overrode any
desire for profit. Yet Otto's comments carried daggers cloaked under a white
veil of repentance. "I realize now that you can't beat the law, no matter how
unjust it may be," Wood lamented, "[and] that is why I have told this story
of my experiences so that others who are tempted to go wrong may see that
you have to pay one way or another for everything you do."[21] Revenue gar-
nered from the sale of the book, the prisoner explained, would "give my two
children some education."[22] A columnist in Raleigh, North Carolina, offered
a review that cited both the positive and negative aspects of *Life History*:

> [Wood] has something for everybody. For the preacher he has a didactic
> message, for the roughneck he has hair-raising experience, and for the
> women he has much love and many marriages. . . . The volume has
> suggestions of humor in it, but Mr. Wood is doing serious business. He
> realizes that popular sentiment is somewhat against him at present,
> but he thinks when the public reads his story of himself it will greatly

relent. This is the really funny thing about his book. He denies the bad things said about him and in the most matter-of-fact way relates the record. For power of understatement Mr. Wood must take the cake.[23]

The press coverage built around the release of Wood's book consistently took a critical stance toward the genuineness of the work's "reformed man" message. "I am through now," Wood countered in an interview. "You have no idea of the tortures a human being suffers when he is being hunted."[24] The noted escapee reassured readers that the book's publication would prevent any further rebellion or chance of escape, especially given the front cover, which distributed his picture "all over the country."[25] "How about putting me to work?" Wood asked prison superintendent George Ross Pou toward the interview's close. "I'll not slip off, honest. You know, solitary is beginning to make me sort of nervous."[26]

Wood's nervousness about living on death row proved not altogether unwarranted. Housed in the cell next to Wood, W. L. Ross, a man from Halifax County, North Carolina, sentenced to death for double murder, frequently sprang into fits of hysteria. On August 5, Ross stuffed himself between two mattresses in his cell and set them on fire. The smoke filled Wood's cell as Ross attempted to burn himself alive. Guards at first ignored Wood's screams for help, having grown used to Ross's outbursts. Eventually realizing that the screams were from Wood, attendants rushed into Ross's cell to stamp out the flames and remove a partially burned yet living Ross from his makeshift pyre.[27] Though Superintendent Pou vehemently protested Wood's release from solitary confinement, the prison board, probably taking into consideration Ross's attempted suicide and the promises Wood laid out in his *Life History*, overruled his pleas. Beginning on September 15, the board allowed Wood to work in the boiler room, an area of the prison that allowed more freedom while limiting avenues of escape.[28]

Two months later, on November 23, 1926, the *Danville Bee* announced the news both expected and feared by state prison superintendent George Ross Pou. "Otto Wood picturesque bandit-murderer and leader of state's prison colony of literature made a clean-cut getaway early [on November 22]," boasted the article's opening sentence.[29] The sarcastic reference to the prison's "colony of literature" referenced the success of Wood's book, which within just a few months had reportedly sold a respectable five hundred copies.[30] This time Wood managed his escape due to a missing latch pin from the prison's rear gate. The mysterious disappearance of a latch pin, coupled with a small gap in the iron grating, allowed the fugitive to

PRICE IS SET ON HEAD OF OUTLAW JAILS CAN'T HOLD

Notorious Bad Man Makes Escape From State Prisons

C.H. (OTTO) WOOD

Clipping from the *Nevada State Journal*, December 31, 1926. (Author's collection)

"squeeze through." The last account of Wood's presence on the prison grounds placed him as "turned out of his cell at 6:30" in the morning to relieve a fireman in the boiler house. Though Wood's escape most likely occurred before daybreak, prison officials failed to detect his absence until almost an hour later, when he missed breakfast. The boiler room fireman later explained that Wood never came to his post.[31]

As the prison staff fanned out in a search of the immediate area, administrators focused their inquiries on the guards stationed at the rear gate.[32] The *Danville Bee* relayed that "the prison guards, J. R. Hux and his brother [Sterling Hux], were changing posts when the 'bad man' made his daybreak 'gate-a-way.'"[33] "Prison inmates," related the *Statesville Landmark*, "had observed Wood in conversation with Hux on several occasions and the guard appeared very friendly towards him."[34] The Hux brothers, under suspicion of complicity in the escape, were charged with gross negligence and promptly fired. By contrast, Superintendent Pou received a recognition from the prison's board of directors, who "publicly absolved . . . [him] of any responsibility in connection with the escape."[35]

With the disappearance, the state of North Carolina slowly awoke to the call for another manhunt for Otto Wood. The event easily caught the attention of the press, which readily advertised a reward of $250 for Wood's capture.[36] "After a day and night of futile search," wrote one columnist, "North Carolina's army of police and county officers today was organized into a giant man-hunting machine with one purpose in view." With the headline "Dragnet for Wood Extends 3 States," the *Danville Bee* noted the huge scale of the search for Wood. "Descriptions of the convict already have been broadcast over the country," the article assured the public.[37]

Despite an early air of urgency within news reports, journalists in North Carolina and Virginia quickly calmed into a steady commentary on yet another of Otto Wood's "vacations." One reporter kidded that Wood escaped "two days ahead of his schedule established last year." The writer declared that the outlaw embodied the traits of the recently deceased Harry Houdini, honoring the famous magician's tricks with his own "usual effective disappearing acts for the edification of the reading citizenry."[38] Another report named Otto "the South's Gerald Chapman," referring to the recently executed Chicago gangster.[39] While numerous comparisons poured from the pens of newshounds, several of their contemporaries seized the opportunity to offer a more in-depth examination of the infamous bandit's character. A writer to the *Statesville Landmark*, under the banner "Here's an Old Familiar," offered a brief examination of the celebrity criminal and placed the 1926 escape within the context of the previous "spectacles":

> Otto Wood just can't abide a Thanksgiving season inside State prison. This is his third escape. Last fall he departed the institution just before Thanksgiving. One of Mr. Wood's temperamental disposition can't be thankful from inside prison walls, and so come the season for returning thanks he craves the open spaces. . . . Recently Wood published a book, or pamphlet, telling of experiences, in which he claimed that he had made a half dozen successful escapes from prison. He warned all and sundry that the straight and narrow was the only proper course and advised against trying the getaway once you were in. It doesn't pay, he said. But it would seem that Otto, like many other writers, was unable to take his own advice.[40]

"Otto Wood Loves the Limelight," proclaimed another article with the subhead "Officers Believe Escaped Prisoner Itches for Publicity and Will Break Out in Spectacular Manner Soon." The column hypothesized that

"Otto Wood may be depended upon to give the tip himself.... Unless some-body runs across him in the meantime, he will break loose some place to let the community know he's about." "That has been the history of Otto Wood," the article continued as the author recounted "wild automobile rides that made his [1924] dash a regular hare and hound race" and "an open motor tour over western North Carolina" in 1925. The journalist further suggested that the desperado would not have broken out of jail without the inten-tion to "break back into print."[41] By the time these words made it to press, a flurry of Otto Wood sightings had already been reported across western North Carolina and southern Virginia.

A report from High Point, North Carolina, claimed that several witnesses saw Otto in the town between 10:30 and 11 a.m. on the day of his escape. The account outlined how three men spotted a suspicious character who matched Wood's description eating at High Point's City Hall café, located "within the shadow of the police station." A member of the trio noticed that "Wood entered the café boldly but kept looking about with cautious eyes and craning his neck to look behind the counter."[42] One week later, a Chase City, Virginia, woman recalled seeing Wood in her hometown on November 27.[43] Practical jokers, determined to make the most of the tense environment surrounding Wood's third escape, called the Greensboro po-lice station with the salutation "This is 'Otto Wood' speaking."[44] Adding to the attention on Greensboro, a Salvation Army worker named William Miller recounted that while working in the state prison, he had spoken with Wood, who made what he termed a "cryptic utterance." "Tell your friends up in Greensboro I'll be up to see them in a few days," Wood had told Miller.[45] On December 3, Danville, Virginia, police attempted to arrest a man who matched Wood's description only to find that he "displayed two good hands and an entire absence of gold-plated molars."[46] The false alarms and phone calls would continue to plague lawmen well into the middle of January 1927.

While Wood maintained a low profile throughout the latter part of 1926, members of the public began to make their opinions known about the noto-rious escapee through interviews, phone calls, and even poetry. In a bizarre phone call to the Greensboro police, an unidentified conspiracy theorist declared that Wood had never even escaped the penitentiary but had been "put away" and killed by prison officials. The man further stated that if Wood "never was put away," he felt that "Otto had been punished enough and that if he came by [his home] ... [Wood] would get a nickel and a hand-out."[47] A Kinston, North Carolina, Baptist congregation took issue not only with Otto's criminal activities but also with his claim to the title of "Most Widely Read Author in the State." That title, the parishioners averred, was held by the Reverend Dr. Bernard W. Spillman, "the foremost authority of the Southern Baptist Church." Winking with sarcasm, the contributing journalist concluded that "Wood and Dr. Spillman as authors have something in common in that both point the way to a better life."[48] With overtures toward comedic poetry, a Virginia writer dubbed "F. C. Betts" offered verse from the perspective of North Carolina's Houdini:

> Sung By Otto Wood.
> I'm on my way from dear old Raleigh today.
> That's why I'm feeling gay;
> I made my gate-a-way [sic] just before Thanksgiving day.
> George Ross Pou, please do not grieve,
> As I had to take French leave.
> Thirty years is a long, long time.
> To stay in Hotel Pou. Some day I'll write you a line.
> Maybe in the good old summer time.—F. C. BETTS[49]

As Virginians waxed poetic, a Greensboro reporter took a small survey of the public opinion about the renegade in his hometown, the site of Wood's one notorious murder: "Whether he just had to spend the Thanksgiving among more familiar and friendly scenes, or decided to increase the sale of his life, published some time ago, is not known—betting was about even on each of these propositions around the city yesterday. And it was somewhat interesting to hear the remarks of those who know much of Wood's career, it being almost a universal sentiment hereabouts that since he was gone, he ought to stay gone by seeking entirely new fields."[50]

The opinions and literature inspired by Wood's third prison break continued to pour in as the fugitive himself remained silent. While some urged Otto to seek "new fields," Winston-Salem resident G. M. "Red" Austin boasted, "There is one man in North Carolina who is not afraid of Otto Wood and that is myself." Austin, whose comments featured prominently in an extended exposé on the bandit's history, married Rushey Hayes after she gained a divorce from Wood in December 1924. The article continued to impart the elaborate tale behind the relationship between Wood and Miss Rushey Hayes, "a typical honest Wilkes county country girl" and "a member of one of Wilkes county's most highly respected families." As the newspaper recounted, the courtship read "like a page out of a book of fiction," in which Wood convinced Miss Hayes that he worked as a traveling salesman while moonlighting as a desperado. In its highly stylized and dramatized portrait of Wood's crimes along the Boone Trail, the article effectively framed Otto Wood's criminal adventures against the backdrop of the Appalachian

Mountains.[51] The journalist who wrote the article was also obviously completely unaware of reports of Wood's wife and child accompanying him on his crime sprees as far away as Texas.

Unwilling to follow the advice to leave North Carolina, Wood broke his silence on December 4, 1926, in a letter from Ashland, Kentucky, to the *Greensboro Daily News*. The outlaw, in a manner deemed by one source as "spectacular as ever," offered terms for his surrender to the state. North Carolina newspapers reprinted the fugitive's proposal for terms of surrender and his statement of grievances:

Ashland, Kentucky, 11-28-26

I guess there are a good many people throughout the state that are very much interested in my whereabouts since my third escape. I haven't went to Australia yet and don't think I will go any ways soon [*sic*]. The reason why I left the state prison is because there is so much difference made between me and the other prisoners. I am the only prisoner that has been locked up in solitary confinement I stayed in solitary one time 10 months, another time seven months and another time five weeks, all told 18 months and one week and it is a living hell. There have been other prisoners that escaped as many as six times; the only punishment they got is C grade. I was even denied the privilege of writing my little children. Other prisoners are allowed to write one and two letters a week.

I won't try and explain the great injustice that I have received at the state prison. I have no desire to remain a fugitive from justice. God knows my heart. I have no desire to break the law and won't until I am forced to. I realize that when a man breaks the law he should be punished. I have been sentenced by the courts of justice to serve 30 years in the state prison and I don't believe any man or woman that were in the court room but what won't say that I got too much time. But I am willing to try and serve the time if I get the chance that other prisoners get.

If the governor would change my sentence to a chaingang [*sic*] or under some superintendent and would assure me that I would be treated human [*sic*] I would give up to Chief Thomas at Winston-Salem within 48 hours after I have been assured that I would not get the torturing that I have got before and that I would be placed on the equal bearing of other prisoners. Personally I hold no dislike for Captain Pou and I will not try and criticize him through the newspapers. I wish him well, but I will try awful hard that he will never get me in his charge anymore. In case the good people wants to take this matter up they can get in touch with me through the newspapers.[52]

Wood's bargaining, coupled with his directly addressing the people of North Carolina, infuriated Superintendent Pou. The warden offered a rapid-fire response to Wood's letter:

We are continuing our efforts to capture Otto Wood and we shall until we have him. . . . The reason we kept him in solitary confinement was because that is the only way he can be kept in any prison, and if he is captured, as long as I have anything to say about it, he will go back to solitary. As to his statement that he would be willing to surrender in 48 hours if he could be assigned to a chaingang [*sic*], that is mere twaddle, for he would not stay on a chaingang [*sic*] longer than 48 hours. He was shown all consideration it was safe to show him while he was here—and results show that he was shown too much as it is. If we catch him alive—and I hope we will—he will certainly go back into solitary confinement. If he is declared an outlaw any citizen of the state will be privileged to capture him, or shoot him on sight.[53]

Governor Angus W. McLean, following a Pou's request, doubled the reward for Wood's capture to $500 and tactfully announced to the public that "a revision of the prison law in 1925 automatically made an escaped convict an outlaw who may be killed by any citizen in the face of resistance."[54] "I will not treat with Otto Wood or any prisoner," McLean declared to his state. "As far as I am concerned he is to be shown no consideration."[55] With Pou and McLean's combined dismissal of Wood's offer, the state of North Carolina decided to take a stand against Otto Wood's rabble-rousing antics.

Officially an outlaw for the third time in his life, Wood's appeal to the people to get in touch with him through newspapers drew ready replies in the early weeks of January 1927. Wood's reference to Australia in his November letter proved that he regularly read the *Greensboro Daily News*, which had printed a lighthearted suggestion that Wood "go to Australia" just two days after his third break.[56] A Greensboro columnist, presumably writing with the knowledge that Wood might read his commentary, chided the state of North Carolina and asked, "How much shall the state set aside for rewards for Otto Wood?" The writer proposed that, since "Otto seems to be good for one escape a year," "he certainly deserves a place on the budget."[57] After another reported sighting of Wood in Kernersville, North Carolina, on January 6, "poet" F. C. Betts once again posted a submission to the *Danville Bee*:

Otto Wood, the slippery North Carolina convict was reported in
    Kernersville last week;
he probably had heard George Ross Pou's song.

He is on his way they say,
To dear old Raleigh today,
He's been nearly two months away,
Spending New Year's and Christmas day,
Since making his get-away.—F.C.B.[58]

Little over a week later, on January 17, 1927, practical jokers called the States-ville police headquarters with a "tip" that Wood "had just left Taylorsville headed for Statesville." Before the officers could ask for further details, the pranksters hung up, leaving Police Chief Tom Kerr and three deputies to wait in vain for Wood's appearance on the highway.[59] Continued pranks and satirical news articles only added to the folk hero popularity of Otto Wood as members of the public joined in the excitement of his latest "vacation."

The fun ended on January 25, 1927, when a Terre Haute, Indiana, druggist fired two shots from a pistol into the chest of a man who was attempting to hold up his shop. Inexplicably, instead of falling dead, the robber ran from the shop, only to have police find him in a nearby boardinghouse three hours later. The failed robber first gave police the name "Edward Hazen," saying he was from Huntington, West Virginia. Hazen was rooming with a twenty-year-old woman who gave her name as Daisy Decker of Owensboro, Kentucky.[60] No doubt noticing the missing left hand, Indiana and federal authorities shortly thereafter identified the severely wounded man as Otto Wood.[61] The bullets had bounced off a change purse full of coins in Wood's left vest pocket, but one had entered the bandit's chest four inches below the heart.[62] Dressed in clothes and a watch stolen from an Indiana railroad brakeman as well as driving a car missing from Roanoke, Virginia, since January 10, Wood now faced a threefold threat: from the state of Indiana, the state of North Carolina, and the federal government. While North Caro-lina lobbied for his return to the state prison, Indiana held Wood for at-tempted armed robbery with a potential sentence of twenty years. Federal authorities also laid claim to Wood, citing his history of car thefts as "inter-state trafficking in stolen automobiles."[63]

While states and the federal government debated Wood's fate, newspa-pers once again waged war over his character. "Many who are inclined to admire Otto Wood are wondering if he did not permit himself to be shot," wrote a *Gastonia Gazette* reporter, continuing, "He has always maintained that he used a gun only as a bluff, and that he has never shot anyone." The journalist reiterated Wood's claim that Kaplan's murder in 1924 resulted from an accident and that "the blow he struck was not hard enough to cause death." By the Gastonia writer's estimation, Wood was not a vicious murderer but a good-natured rogue endowed with a "particular type of criminal insanity—a sort of 'escapomaniac'—whose greatest thrill is to get in prison and then get out."[64] A less sympathetic columnist countered that the "Otto kind are hopeless" and offered a brief and, ultimately, prophetic message: "The result is history. If and when Otto is returned and kept in close confinement after awhile there will arise a complaint from criminal sympathizers. They will say that he is being killed by degrees. . . . But the criminal sympathizers are always asking for them to have a chance, notwithstanding they take up their old tricks the moment they are given a fraction of liberty."[65]

A week after Wood's wounding, North Carolina won the custody battle. On February 18, 1927, Wood, miraculously able to walk, manacled to a North Carolina State Prison guard, boarded a train headed south back to confinement in Raleigh. On a stopover in Cincinnati, an Ohio reporter questioned the captured outlaw about the motivations behind his third escape. "Every man is entitled to a little vacation," Wood responded.[66] On reaching Raleigh, Superintendent Pou returned Wood to solitary confinement on death row.[67]

After a visit to Wood's death row cell, politely termed the "Safe Keeping" quarters by prison officials, on February 22, 1927, a Raleigh correspondent reported that the man "notorious for more fact and fable than any other Tar Heel escapist" slumbered in comfortable conditions. As the writer explained, Wood, "the only occupant of death row without an ordained funeral day," lived in an electric-lit cell with furniture that "does not fulfill its dread implications."[68] During the Raleigh reporter's visit, prison officials publicly expressed their disbelief at "the volume of mail coming to the prison from sentimentalists all over the state." An article titled "Flappers Weep for Otto Wood" noted that Wood's fans consisted predominantly of young women who wrote to protest the conditions that Wood suffered while in prison. In response, Superintendent Pou prohibited Wood from writing to newspapers or giving interviews. News stories reported that, in contrast to his publicized refusal of leniency, Pou showed some ability to relent in the face of Wood's fan mail and promised to weigh the option of removing the outlaw from solitary confinement to work on a rock-busting gang.[69] The superintendent probably rethought bending to the public's will when Wood attacked death row guard Evander McKeenan on April 30. After a short brawl, McKeenan restrained the one-handed convict and carried him back to his cell. Perhaps knowing the fight ruined any chance of his release from solitary, Wood cursed Pou and the rest of the prison from behind the bars.[70]

Pou's authority may have kept Wood from publishing any further pleas to North Carolina's populace, but the criminal's statewide popularity proved hard to suppress. "Sales from his first book continue to pile up," bragged the *Statesville Landmark*. "His escape gave good advertising to the little volume . . . which stands out as the best seller among North Carolina literary productions."[71] A story from Thomasville, North Carolina, relayed the news that a robber who "described himself as Otto Wood's brother" held up taxis in the area and claimed "he was on his way to Raleigh to open the state prison and liberate his 'brother.'"[72] Though in reality no relation to Wood, this thief's claim of kinship proved disturbing to Carolina lawmen as they tried unsuccessfully to squelch the spread of the "escapomaniac's" notoriety. North Carolina State College joined in the Otto Wood phenomena with an April Fool's edition of their weekly newspaper, *The Technician*, in which students named Otto Wood "champion cross-country man of North Carolina."[73] The University of North Carolina's *Daily Tar Heel* listed Wood, under the title "Little Squirt," as a member of the mock campus organization "The Imperial Order of Booloos."[74] An even more peculiar proposition to cash in on Wood's fame came from a sideshow entrepreneur who offered to rent the convict from the penitentiary and display him on tour in a cage. Shocked by the sincerity of the showman's offer, Superintendent Pou and Dr. J. H. Norman, the state prison physician, declined what the exhibitionist termed "a good chance to make some money."[75]

By the end of the summer of 1927, Otto Wood's celebrity throughout the state appeared to reach record appeal. In a brief fall interview, no doubt gleaned without the blessing of Superintendent Pou, Wood proudly announced that he had "disposed of about 1,000 copies of his book." Despite the success, Wood stated that he "[did] not intend to do any more writing any time soon." The reporter described the bandit's cell as "literally covered with newspapers" that kept him aware of events outside the prison. With political tact, Wood declared his belief in capital punishment, with the caveat that "the guilt of anyone should always be proven before he is sent down the line to the chair."[76]

Wood reappeared in the news six months later, in May 1928, when noted evangelist Billy Sunday visited death row. Stopping by Wood's cell, Sunday made a point of speaking with North Carolina's most noted escape artist. "I'd like to become a Christian if I could be sincere about it," Wood told the reverend, "but under the circumstances I don't see how I can." Noticing that Wood fed sparrows that flew to the barred window of his cell, Sunday decided to take a chance and preach Wood a sermon. "Those birds have faith in you, they know you won't harm them," Sunday urged. "If you had the same faith in God, He will save you." Negotiations for Wood's soul broke down after Sunday told Wood to follow the prison rules. Wood argued:

"Why Mr. Sunday, I don't break the rules except that I do go home . . . once in a while." Before leaving Wood's cell, Sunday asked Wood if he believed in capital punishment. Wood reiterated his belief that "I don't believe a man should be given a death sentence on circumstantial evidence." Wood had likely heard Sunday praying with another death row prisoner, John Clyburn. Clyburn, a black man convicted of murder in Charlotte, North Carolina, was sentenced to death primarily due to the testimony of another prisoner who had been given a temporary stay of execution.[77] In this case, it seems Wood may have been using his celebrity to direct Sunday and the press to take notice of cases such as Clyburn's.

The cell-bound interviews of 1927 and 1928 signaled a victory in Wood's campaign to gain public sympathy. With a large section of people statewide convinced of his mistreatment under the law, Wood had arrived as North Carolina's most notable criminal celebrity. Within a year, a push toward reform-minded politics brought on by a new administration in North Carolina's highest office would further solidify Wood's status as public figure. Wood, the Houdini, would soon become a political pawn, a poster child for social reform in the state of North Carolina.

CHAPTER 6

AN EXPERIMENT IN HUMANITY

THE REFORMER AND THE RENEGADE,

1928–1930

They brought him back and got him well
And locked him into a dungeon cell
And there he stayed for days and days
Until he promised he'd change his ways
—"Otto Wood, the Bandit," recorded by Slim Smith, Victor
    Records 67436-1, February 5, 1931, New York, New York

"Tho' OTTO WOOD seems no good, Raleigh can't keep him if she would,"
pipes Prof MacBetts, commenting on the prisoner's last getaway.
—*Danville Bee*, July 17, 1930

We say with the Wilmington Star after hearing that [Wood] was
"seen" in California, "that there are two kinds of wood in California,
Redwood and Otto Wood."
—"An Otto Wood Scare," *The Robesonian* (Lumberton, NC),
    September 18, 1930

All hell could not make Otto honorable.
—*Mt. Airy (NC) News*, July 17, 1930

IN JULY 1930, mill hand John Lewis Powell sauntered his way through
the midsummer heat of the North Carolina Piedmont, searching for
work. Misfortune seemed to follow Powell: a car accident only a few
years before had left him with a crippled left arm and noticeable limp in
his left leg. When the cotton mill that employed him closed, Powell decided
to walk and hitchhike his way south from Richmond, Virginia, to Atlanta,
Georgia, hoping mills there might provide employment. Heading south
through the Carolinas, the unfortunate hitchhiker made slow progress,
halted by police a total fifteen times between Richmond and Spartanburg,
South Carolina, alone. As he bathed his road-worn feet in a stream near

Charlotte, North Carolina, Powell found himself surrounded by five police-men, who took him at gunpoint to the city jail. Releasing him the next day, the officers explained that they had mistaken his identity. By the time Pow-ell reached Spartanburg, he was prepared. As a patrolman pulled his car to a stop, Powell took a photograph and a letter from the police chief of Gasto-nia, North Carolina, from his pocket. Holding up the picture, the mill hand once again explained that he was indeed not Otto Wood.[1]

Powell's story, reprinted in newspapers across the South, was among the most popular tales of misidentifications made by police as they searched for the whereabouts of North Carolina's best-known escape artist. The witch hunt that victimized Powell constituted a minor incident in the hysteria that surrounded Wood's fourth flight from the North Carolina State Prison in Raleigh. The heightened intensity of the manhunt owed much to the events that occurred in the year before the escape. After two years of silence in solitary confinement, Wood had reemerged in the summer of 1929 with the help of a political ally: an entrepreneurial governor whose penchant for publicity inadvertently set the stage for the Carolina desperado's final run.

Inaugurated as governor of North Carolina in January 1929, Oliver Max Gardner's background made him well acquainted with the environment that produced Otto Wood. The son of a Civil War veteran and country doc-tor Oliver Perry "OP" Gardner, "O' Max" lost his mother at the age of ten and spent much of his childhood on house calls with his father in and around Shelby, in Cleveland County, North Carolina. In his travels with OP, the younger Gardner saw firsthand the plight of the rural poor within his home state. Among the sayings passed to Gardner from his father was one that directly influenced his attitude toward criminals—that "ignorance was the mother of poverty and the grandmother of crime."[2] Gardner kept this quote in mind as he entered into the governorship and demanded reforms within the practices of the state prison system. "The object of our penal system is, in part, to bring about reformation," stated Gardner in a 1928 stump speech. He declared the need for improvements in education, particularly for "young boys, even though they may be inclined toward a life of crime."[3] Governor Gardner intended to reshape the state from the bottom up, real-izing his vision of North Carolina as a socially progressive state, rich in its humanity.

The new administration under Gardner recognized that the state prison system constituted a key battleground in their attempt to modernize the state of North Carolina. Gardner and his constituents believed that by ini-tiating a concentrated, highly publicized campaign to reform prisoners by vocation and education rather than by punishment, they could demonstrate the power of their populist approach to social issues. In his first biennial address to the North Carolina General Assembly, Gardner stated the need for "a modern plant" to replace "the unsafe, costly, unsanitary, and wholly inadequate central prison." He further suggested that the state set up more sanitary prison farms where the inmates could practice the production of foodstuffs and thus act as beneficiaries to their fellow citizens through agriculture. Six months after this address, Gardner ordered prisoners removed from work leases to the Carolina Coal Company, which previously had brought an annual revenue of $90,000 to the penitentiary. The action came as the result of accidents including electrocution, elevator malfunctions, and a prisoner crushed by a coal car. Gardner advised that the prison board loan their inmate population to construction jobs less hazardous to their safety, specifically to the building of roads and highways—another of his pet projects for the improvement of the Tar Heel State.[4]

Under the supervision of Gardner's administration, the North Carolina State Board of Charities and Public Welfare published a pamphlet on both the historical and contemporary problems of crime and punishment in the Old North State. Titled *Capital Punishment in North Carolina*, the report selected twenty-six death row prisoners to profile in criminal case studies that compiled their various backgrounds, mental states, and personal histories. A majority of the prisoners profiled were black men, and nearly all were from impoverished backgrounds. Otto Wood (listed as "Case E"), despite only being on death row for solitary confinement, featured prominently in the study. The report contained an in-depth examination of Wood's personality:

> The prisoner is rather histrionic but shows some finesse. He walks into an audience with a somewhat self-important air, seems perfectly at ease, talks frankly, does not show any unusual emotional reaction, is neat in his appearance. . . . He talks rather loudly, using incorrect English, but trying to use impressive words and phrases. . . . He has very definite wanderlust; and Jesse James type of hereditary criminal propensities. He expresses himself as being entirely fearless—and the examiner believes he is. . . . He seems to be unmoral and unsocial rather than immoral and anti-social, and these characteristics, it is believed, developed partly out of his native endowment and partly out of his environmental influences. He is an extrovert of a pronounced type, and is willing to make any decision, take any chance, or do anything the occasion requires, on a moment's notice. He expresses sorrow for having done wrong immediately afterwards, but this remorse, if it may be called remorse, quickly leaves him and he will do the same thing or

worse upon the next occasion. . . . If one had to be bound by a definite psychiatric opinion, he might be put down as a mild hypomaniac [*sic*].[5]

The bulletin also offered the supposition that Wood, despite his reported physical age of thirty-three, possessed a mental age of ten years and four months. The results of the study produced a profile rife with inconsistencies that painted Wood as a "hypersexed," nonalcoholic ex-bootlegger suspected to suffer from "early locomoter ataxia" (jerky body movement/paralysis) due to spinal syphilis.[6] Despite the bizarre conclusions—how exactly was a man with a mental age of around ten years able to function as a hypersexed bootlegger?—due to flaws in early psychiatric science, the characteristics attributed to Wood in *Capital Punishment* melded into a portrait of a victim. Though they labeled him "unmoral and unsocial," the authors of *Capital Punishment* depicted Wood as someone who had fallen into criminal activity due to circumstances extending back to his childhood years.

The findings about Otto Wood and his fellow convicts within *Capital Punishment in North Carolina*, gleaned mostly from primitive psychiatric observations and from personal interviews, supported Governor Gardner's social reform message, which stressed improving education and combatting poverty as ways to suppress crime. The pamphlet's introduction featured an array of language suitable to Gardner's platform:

> The prisoners in death row are there because the people of North Carolina wish them to be or are indifferent to or ignorant of the social factors responsible for their situation. . . .
>
> [A citizen] will see among these condemned men the poor and the ignorant—for the affluent and educated are seldom found in the death cells—the feeble-minded, the insane and the psychopathic. By talking to them he will discover that some of them are so simple in mind that they have little conception of the seriousness of their situation. . . .
>
> [A citizen] may be led to wonder whether there may not be children in his own community who are starting on the same path, and if so, whether he cannot do something about it. And if these impressions give him a feeling of responsibility, the purpose of this study will have been largely accomplished. . . . The North Carolina State Board of Charities and Public Welfare hopes thereby to stimulate a sane, popular interest in a tragic human problem, from which, it is hoped, will come an enlarged social program of prevention.[7]

With the burden of North Carolina's crime wave placed on the shoulders of the public, Gardner continued his crusade with visits to the state prison in Raleigh. In July 1929, Wood and Gardner came face-to-face during one of the governor's tours of the Central Prison facilities. The shackled man who greeted Gardner bore little resemblance to the wily criminal previously described in newspaper accounts. Instead, the inmate seemed a gaunt, frail figure shriveled by two years on death row with no outside exercise. Observing Wood's condition and listening to his coughing fits convinced Gardner that the convict could no longer stay confined on death row.[8] Released to back into the general population of the prison, Wood reportedly regained twelve pounds within the course of several weeks.[9]

By late July, a Raleigh reporter noted that the sharp change in Wood's living conditions, mainly too "much freedom and food," had put him in the prison hospital for a short stay. Calling Wood "Greensboro's most illustrious literarian [*sic*] since that city lost O. Henry and Wilbur Daniel Steel," the reporter intimated that the convict's illness was a minor reaction after he "ate too much food for his own good and was stricken down with something akin to acute indigestion."[10] Not willing to take chances, prison warden and physician Dr. J. H. Norman—whose car Wood had used to make his escape in 1924—ordered staff to secure all doors and protect the furniture in the prison hospital, leaving Wood no opportunities to break out.[11] While prison officials waited for Wood to recover, planning to send their perpetual fugitive to the road gang in Bladen County, located in the southeastern corner of the state, Governor Gardner considered a different course of action.[12] The governor saw an opportunity in publicizing the reformation of North Carolina's most noted criminal. As Wood lay in the prison hospital, Gardner mulled the idea of using the "Houdini of Cell Block A" as a poster child in his fight to restructure the North Carolina prison system.

Although the prison reform movement showed signs of gaining a potential figurehead, Gardner's attempts to reform the state outside the prison walls met a substantial number of stumbling blocks. The most notable of these, the Loray Mill strike in Gastonia, brought national attention to the Old North State and challenged the governor's progressive image with an outbreak of violence as cotton mill workers protested for better conditions and wages. The onset of the Great Depression in the fall of 1929 also added to the strain as Gardner scrambled to balance the implementation of new programs with the struggle to prevent economic collapse. Within his first year in office, he had diverted $6.5 million to improving school systems in the state's most impoverished areas. The governor also diverted an additional $1.25 million to the easement of property taxes, a gesture that catered to farmers in the poorest counties recorded for 1929. By the fall of 1929, however, the nationwide bank crisis affected the state and jeopardized the

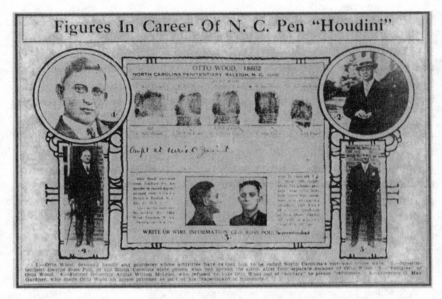

Illustration accompanying an article by C. R. Sumner in the
Asheville Citizen-Times, September 7, 1930. Sumner produced several
stories on Wood in the bandit's final years. (Author's collection)

feasibility of any further large-scale programs. In 1930 alone, ninety-three
North Carolina banks with deposits of over $56 million closed. In an effort
to alleviate the early strains suffered by Carolinians under the Depression,
Gardner promoted such morale-building events as "live-at-home" days, held
throughout the week of December 15–21, 1929. The week celebrated self-
sufficiency among the public and invited statewide pride through meals
that featured only "products from North Carolina farms."[13] Through these
efforts, Gardner displayed the same magnanimous personality and penchant for showmanship that served as his hallmark approach to political
reform.

In the early months of 1930, Otto Wood displayed a character suitable
enough to validate Governor Gardner's progressive approach to correctional
institutions.[14] In the wake of Gardner's visit, in summer 1929, Wood had
become a model prisoner, indulging in activities such as the management
of a prison delicatessen and canteen; he was eventually assigned the title
Assistant Keeper of the Prison Canteen.[15] Wood also collaborated with
William Campbell, fellow inmate (and convicted murderer), to maintain a
small animal collection, which the press referred to as the "Carolina State

Prison Zoo." The collection of animals—housed somewhere in the prison—reportedly included "white rats, a Texas ant bear, chinchillas, monkeys, a groundhog, snakes, foxes, a goat . . . an Airdale [sic] dog, rabbits and cats," all purchased with the help of funds from Wood's proceeds at the soft drink stand.[16] A report on Wood's condition in October 1929 depicted him as "well pleased" and eager to keep his job in charge of the prison delicatessen, where "he tells all who come within his range that he is satisfied these days."[17] Wood's actions suggested that he possessed no reason to make any further runs from justice and desired to live up to the wholesome image Gardner needed from him.

On May 20, 1930, Wood gained further recognition when he received the classification of an "Honor Grade" or "A Grade" prisoner, reinstated with the maximum number of privileges afforded behind bars. With subtle fanfare, Gardner personally knighted Wood with his "A" grade, declaring Wood an "experiment in humanity."[18] The *Wilkes Journal-Patriot* printed a column describing Wood's promotion: "Otto Wood, once the toughest guy by his own admonition in the North Carolina state penitentiary, Tuesday took his place among 'honor grade' prisoners, softened by the kindly acts of a chief executive who was, as Otto said, 'willing to give a guy a break.' . . . Governor Gardner had a talk with Otto. He promised him better quarters and a chance to exercise if he would promise in turn not to break jail. Otto promised."[19] The *Asheville Citizen-Times* later reprinted the speech Gardner gave to Wood in front of the press: "I am going to take a chance with you and see if a man who has gone as far downhill as you have can go back up. I want to warn you that if you escape again the ray of hope will cease to burn for many other prisoners and that if you make good it will mean that others will get a chance too."[20] In response to Gardner's speech, Wood told the governor, "I won't offer you my word of honor, because that wouldn't be much; but you can be sure of one thing, I'll never run away as long as you are Governor."[21] With one brief statement, Wood became Gardner's self-created monster, an experiment fully envisioned yet ultimately difficult to control.

As the press largely celebrated Gardner's decision to promote Wood to an A-grade prisoner, the publicity surrounding the event proved troubling to several commentators. Recalling the success and popularity of Wood's *Life History*, one Statesville columnist remarked on Wood's selling his "goodness" to the public before his 1926 escape, intimating that this well-publicized event might produce the same result. "Mr. Wood's book showed him to be a very fine man," the writer stated, tongue hard in cheek. "Nobody ever had a less murderous heart and he proved to a great many people he never killed Kaplan of Greensboro."[22] Though he had been reconstructed as a model to his fellow prisoners and the public of North Carolina, Wood's constant desire for more elbow room almost instantly outweighed his dedication to reform.

Shortly after 6 p.m. on July 10, 1930, Governor Gardner received notification from state prison warden H. H. Honeycutt that Otto Wood had escaped—a fact noticed after the prisoner failed to report for evening lockup. A massive net hastily formed by guards around the prison grounds failed to ensnare Wood, and soon an all-out panic of radio, telephone, and telegraph reports surged nationwide.[23] When asked to comment on his Wood's escape, Gardner lamented: "I do not regret releasing him from solitary confinement, but I do regret his betrayal of my trust in trying to treat him humanely as other prisoners at State's prison are."[24] In another interview, Gardner expressed "confidence that the wily convict would be captured" and afterward sent to the Caledonia Prison Farm. Acknowledging Wood's past escapes from convict road gangs, Gardner remarked that Otto would definitely not see service as a water boy, since "it's too far to the springs."[25] Despite his outward display of confidence, Gardner knew the escape signaled a major setback in his campaign intent to reform the state prison system.

Writing a year after the escape, one prison official noted: "The shrewd mind of Otto Wood had planned and carried into effect an escape that still remains a mystery." The official account released by the North Carolina State Prison could only acknowledge that they last saw Otto in the prison at around noon on the day of his escape.[26] In trying to piece together how Wood managed to exit the stockade in Raleigh, prison officials determined that either Celia Wood, Otto's sister-in-law, or a woman named Vera Ellis, both of whom had visited Wood frequently in the last year, had assisted him in breaking out.[27] Detectives later found that an unidentified woman, likely either Ellis or Celia Wood, tried to remove all of the money Wood had earned while in prison from his account in a Raleigh bank.[28] Despite no concrete evidence on how Wood got beyond the prison grounds, sources later indicated that prison guard David Massey, whose car Wood stole after exiting the prison, changed the usual parking place of his car on the day of Wood's escape. Even more damning to Massey's reputation, the guard quit working for the prison shortly after Wood stole his car. Whether Massey was simply in the wrong place at the wrong time or a key player in Wood's getting beyond the prison walls has ultimately never been confirmed or denied.[29]

"Prison Walls Do Not a Prison Make for Otto Wood," boasted one headline over a grainy picture of Wood, a wide smirk on his face.[30] While the topic of Wood's fourth escape became front-page news nationwide, North Carolina journalists once again traded assessments of Wood's infamous popularity. "He does not have the imagination of the public as he once did," a Raleigh columnist acknowledged, adding a cynical commentary on both Wood and his fellow North Carolinians: "[Wood] has been advertised too much. He has written a book too and North Carolina people do not like men who write books."[31] In an editorial titled "Hope He Stays Away," the *Statesville Landmark* critiqued Governor Gardner and his experiment. The Statesville columnist politely berated Gardner's well-publicized attempt to redeem Otto and voiced skepticism about his overall approach to prison reform:

> [North Carolinians] are more than anxious to experiment with [Otto Wood]. Our folks have tried and failed signally. . . . It is a conceit of some people who think they can transform criminals by kindness to attach too much importance to their personality. . . . Governor Gardner had a good purpose. He had learned something by his experiment that will be profitable. There is no objection here to these experiments but we're hoping that if Wood comes back, or other prisoners are used as experiments, that the procedure will be carried out with a maximum of quiet and a minimum of parade and glorification. Otto Wood has been paraded and played up until he was no doubt convinced he was a hero. . . . That wasn't kindness to Otto; and the parading of such people is entirely too common down Raleigh way, wasn't good for their mental health nor the mental health of criminals generally. We're strong for the kindness business within bounds. But the semi-hero stuff, the constant playing up of some convict by the Raleigh news writers, somewhat of a habit with them, produces a great weariness in many people; and that is one reason we hope Wood will keep going.[32]

The Statesville columnist reiterated the disapproval of the state's handling of Wood in a September article. "Seeing that our folks have shown themselves incapable of handling this criminal desperado," opined the *Landmark* writer, "there was a general hope that [Otto Wood] would stay away." Despite this hope, the reporter acknowledged that Wood's affinity for the "limelight" and "the thrill he gets from exhibition" made the bandit's reappearance in North Carolina inevitable.[33] The sentiments of the Statesville reporter displayed a weariness with Otto Wood among a contingent of North Carolinians. Though still a popular figure, Wood, a featured criminal within newspapers for nearly twenty years, had seemingly overstayed his welcome. The hope that he "would stay away" became an oft-repeated catch phrase as his fourth flight from prison extended through the remainder of 1930.

Mugshot from the North Carolina State Prison, ca. 1930,
as printed in *Life History of Otto Wood*. (Author's collection)

Reports of Wood's movements after his escape flooded newspapers throughout the summer of 1930. "Has Otto Wood Passed This Way?" asked a Statesville reporter after a gas station robbery in Iredell County. Although never definitively connected with Wood, the crime displayed hallmarks in line with Wood's earlier mode of operation as a highwayman. The station owner, Ed Moore, reported that three men had held him up at gunpoint. When Moore tried to defend himself, two of the men forced him into a car, driving toward Statesville two miles before robbing him and leaving him on the roadside.[34] Desperate to find Otto Wood, police throughout the Carolinas profiled anyone with the same physical handicaps as the homegrown desperado. Most notable among the cases of mistaken identity was John Lewis Powell, a millworker whose limp and maimed left hand caused him to have no less than fifteen run-ins with police officers as he walked along North Carolina's highways.[35]

Adding to the frenzied air surrounding Wood's fourth escape, the mention of the bandit's name on the streets of Greensboro caused a bare-fisted brawl. E. L. Kaplan, son of Abraham Kaplan, killed by Wood in 1924, fought with rival pawnbroker Curley Stack after Stack mentioned Otto Wood in an argument. The two traded blows in the street; a gun pulled by one of Kaplan's friends ensured that no one came to Stack's aid. Kaplan, Stack, and their companions who attempted to join the fight all paid fines to the city for their public display of violence.[36] The scuffle between Kaplan and Stack illustrated how Wood's name, used as a joke by some, was no longer a laughing matter, especially to those directly affected by his crimes.

In mid-July 1930 a Raleigh column, relayed in the *Anniston (AL) Star*, reported the disappearance of the bandit's widowed sister-in-law, Celia (Byrd) Wood, a frequent visitor to Wood in Raleigh and suspected to have aided Wood in fleeing from the penitentiary.[37] A follow-up to the story on Byrd posited that the missing widow eloped with Wood and the duo were now on a trip through several western states. Letters received by Celia's mother traced the couple as they traveled through "Missouri, New Mexico, and . . . California." When asked for a comment, Mrs. Byrd remarked, "My daughter is well thought of and I do not believe she would stay with a man to whom she was not married."[38]

A September 19, 1930, story from High Point, North Carolina, heralded the return of Otto Wood to the Tar Heel State. Under the headline "Otto Wood and Paramour Kidnap Child from High Point School," the *Wilkes Journal-Patriot* relayed an intense tale that delved deep into the affairs of Wood's family. After a night at the Arthur Hotel in High Point, Wood and Byrd traveled to the Grimes Street School to pick up Celia's two daughters, Lucile, age six, and Pansy, age eleven. While Lucile agreed to accompany the couple, Pansy refused and declared her wish to stay with the Byrds, the grandparents who had looked after the children in Celia's absence. The newspaper printed part of Pansy's deposition: "I saw Otto sitting out front in an automobile and asked mama if that was not Uncle Otto. . . . She told me it was a taxi cab driver. But I know Uncle Otto and I know it was him." The columnist recounted how Pansy Wood burst into tears after recounting the events to police. W. P. Byrd, Celia's father, issued an equally emotional call for the law to bring Wood to justice and challenged the state to offer a higher reward for his capture:

> It seems to me the state would be more interested than it seems in getting Otto back in prison. Every state official knows [Wood] is a dangerous man. I do not care so much about my daughter going away with him. If she was crazy enough to go that was her business. She is grown and old enough to know better. But I do hate to think of my little grandaughter [sic] with him, using her to help him get away with his mean tricks. . . .

There is no doubt about him bein armed. He always goes prepared for an emergency. He will attempt a holdup before the first of the week. He must get money from some place and he can't earn it honestly. . . . I just dread to think of my little grandchild being with them I am afraid she is going to get killed. I wish the state would get into this case and get back for me the little girl. . . . It is the duty of North Carolina to go after Otto and I hope state officials will realize the duty.[39]

Details emerged that Otto and Celia Wood traveled "heavily armed" alongside another fugitive from the state: Bill Payne, a bank robber and bootlegger, known to operate in western and central North Carolina. Payne, who had also escaped from the state prison several years earlier, stayed at the Arthur Hotel with Wood and Byrd under an assumed name. "Any attempt to stop them will be very dangerous," warned a report, "for they [the police] know Payne will try to shoot his way out. He has such a reputation and there is no question what Otto will do when cornered."[40] With police connecting Wood with Payne, known for his ruthless tactics and willingness to kill when confronted by police, public sympathy for Wood, already wavering, fell to a new low.

The 1930s constituted a new decade, one with a sense of instability that did not bode well for Wood's prospects as a fugitive. Although newspapers still acknowledged Wood's colorful qualities with nicknames and phantom imagery—using monikers like North Carolina's "will-o'-the-wisp"—concern began to build that Wood no longer exhibited the same playful demeanor that hallmarked his earlier escapes.[41] Governor Gardner and the state's failure to acknowledge Wood as a threat and the inability of officers to quickly corner Wood proved common themes within Carolina newspapers. Although Wood had often denied his portrayal as a bloodthirsty killer, the social climate of 1930, influenced by the Great Depression, gave a heightened sense of desperation to his run. Wood himself more than likely felt the strain of the economic downturn, which had occurred during his time behind bars. With less money to steal, the people of North Carolina proved even less likely to forgive a robber purported to prey on roadside businesses.

Almost in response to Warden Honeycutt's prophecy, a rash of Otto Wood sightings extended across the central and western portions of North Carolina and Virginia throughout September 1930. F. F. Reid, a traveling salesman, contacted the Winston-Salem police force for a photograph of Wood, claiming that the outlaw had robbed him and stolen his car in Roanoke, Virginia. Reid and his wife had found themselves stopped while driving through Roanoke, robbed at gunpoint of $25, a watch, and their car.[42] Soon thereafter, police found the car of former North Carolina State Prison guard David Massey within the city limits of Roanoke, all but confirming Wood as the person who waylaid the Reids.[43]

Wood apparently traveled south after his rush through Roanoke. In North Carolina, Forsyth County officers briefly cornered a man who matched Wood's description between Rural Hall and Winston-Salem, yet failed to capture the suspect when he leaped from his car and escaped.[44] Another report claimed that an Iredell County man saw Wood as the fugitive rode through Statesville, headed west toward Hickory. Jack Little, a local man on his way to work at a furniture factory, identified Wood at a Statesville traffic light. Little remembered that Wood rode in the rumble seat of a car, occupied in its cab by a man and a woman, likely Payne and Celia Byrd. The witness told police of the slightly humorous scene as Wood, knowing that he was recognized, tried to pull a blanket over his head, lifting a small black dog from the seat beside him close to his face until the car pulled away. Little told police that he had previously seen Wood while the bandit was in jail at Mooresville several years earlier and had no doubt that Wood was the person he saw in Statesville.[45] On September 18, an Asheville barber reported giving a man missing his left hand a shave and a haircut, casually discussing how the man was able to drive with only one hand. The barber identified his client as Otto Wood after seeing a photograph.[46] A few days later, the staff at a High Point lunch counter claimed that Wood and "Mrs. Robert Wood, his alleged travelling companion" visited and ate at the stand on September 24. A Mrs. Kenney, a manager, recounted that Celia Byrd came into the counter looking for a place to change her dress. Kenney also made a point to relay that Otto had ordered a ham sandwich, but switched his order to banana after the staff told him that they only had country ham.[47]

For every detailed, confirmed encounter with Otto Wood and his entourage, the press had just as many false leads to report as Wood bounded over the highways and slipped in and out of cities. Police in Fairmont, Robeson County, North Carolina, arrested a door-to-door salesman who looked like Wood, releasing the man after determining that his "description failed to tally with Otto in several respects."[48] Raleigh police reported finding a check "made out to Otto Wood" on "the floor of a local hotel," but acknowledged the discovery as a false alarm and a practical joke.[49] As the reports of sightings streamed in to authorities across the state, lawmen scrambled to catch up with the outlaw, whose sporadic appearances made him nearly impossible to pin down.

North Carolina issued a proclamation on October 9, 1930, that for the fourth time officially dubbed Wood an outlaw, levying a price of $250 for his death or capture.[50] The state prison added an additional $125 to the dead or alive bounty. Governor Gardner, still convinced Wood was not worthy of the term "outlaw," lobbied against the placement of such high rewards for his failed experiment and insisted that more publicity would only fuel the momentum of the fugitive's run.[51] State prison warden Honeycutt reminded Carolinians that "Otto is such a publicity hound [that] if he thought he would get a big headline in the papers he would try almost anything . . . he is pretty shrewd and may give us a lot more trouble."[52]

Just under a month after the state levied the price on Wood's head, on October 25, 1930, authorities in Tulsa, Oklahoma, took into a custody a couple and their six-year-old daughter after finding them sleeping in a car on the roadside. The man, missing his left hand, gave the officer the name "E. J. Pardue." The report later given to North Carolina officials by Tulsa's chief of detectives, Earl A. Franks, described how the effects of the Depression had made it harder to pinpoint highwaymen like Otto Wood: "This man," Chief Franks wrote, "did not have any money and, as it is nothing unusual to find families sleeping in cars under present unemployment conditions, I did not think anything unusual regarding this." After booking Pardue, taking the vagrant's picture, Franks released the family, only to find several hours later that Pardue's mugshot matched that of Otto Wood.[53]

Although unknown to anyone at the time, Detective Franks had encountered Wood on the way back from the western states to North Carolina. Returning just in time for Christmas, the outlaw would visit his relatives and retread his old haunts around the western parts of the Old North State as well as in Virginia and West Virginia. This time, however, Wood's refusal to keep a low profile ultimately proved to be his downfall. The result left bloodstains on the streets of one North Carolina city.

CHAPTER 7

I'LL MAKE 'EM EARN THEIR REWARD

FINAL DAYS, DECEMBER 1930

It is simply a matter of self-defense for the public that one of the
Wood type be killed and the sooner that is done the better.
—*Statesville (NC) Record and Landmark*, January 5, 1931

Mr. Will Rogers, Hollywood, California,
    Otto Wood, Carolina outlaw and will-o-wisp in sensational es-
capes from the state prison . . . arrived in a stolen automobile from
your hometown, Claremore, Oklahoma. Thinking perhaps only citizen of Claremore able to own car might be you, want to render our
usual service by sending you this information.
—Chamber of Commerce [Salisbury, NC]—*Salisbury Post*,
    January 3, 1931

He rambled out West and he rambled all around.
He met two sheriffs in a southern town
And the sheriff says, "Otto! Step to the way!
'Cause I been expecting you every day."
—"Otto Wood the Bandit," recorded by the Carolina Buddies,
    Columbia 151345-2, February 24, 1931, New York, New York

CONSTABLE GEORGE HOLLAND'S car carved ruts in the muddy
road just outside Wilkesboro, North Carolina. His wheels spinning
in the mire, Holland peered through the windshield, his headlights
illuminating a Ford car on the roadside immediately up ahead. Pulling to
a stop just alongside the Ford, the constable heard a familiar voice. "Hello,
George." Holland instantly recognized Otto Wood as he appeared suddenly
in the window displaying a .45 caliber pistol. Feigning small talk, Wood
asked what Holland thought of the gun. The constable responded that it
looked like "a good one." "George, you are not going to try to take me, are
you?" Otto asked. Holland saw the shadowed outlines of several men inside the car behind Wood. "No," the constable replied. Wood then hailed

the men in the car, telling them: "George was a good fellow and ought to have a drink." A quart of whiskey materialized, and Wood tried to convince Holland to take a sip. Refusing the drink and looking for avenues of escape, Holland could see another man standing behind Wood, a pistol in each hand. Likely satisfied that he had startled the constable enough, Wood allowed Holland to drive away. Constable Holland then fought his way through the mud-choked roads, desperate to find the first stop with a telephone. Wilkes County had to know that Otto Wood, their outlaw neighbor, was back home.[1]

Wood's return to North Carolina in December 1930 shared much in common with his movements during previous escapes. The requisite joyride around Wilkes County, during which Wood came face-to-face with Constable Holland, was just one of ways in which the outlaw made his presence known. Although Wood still exhibited his hallmark rowdiness and devil-may-care attitude, he must have felt a change in the people around him. Wood—hardly the mentally underdeveloped ten-year-old mind profiled by prison psychiatrists—must have seen firsthand the effects brought on by the onset of the Great Depression as he traveled to and from the West. Whether or not the sights of dispossessed families sleeping in their cars, massive numbers of unemployed people walking the highways, or railyards full of bums had any effect on Wood is unknown. What is clear is that Otto either chose to ignore the Depression altogether or embraced the nationwide feeling of gradually building despair and decided to be even more bold in his crimes and carousing. Whatever the truth, the wheels were already in motion for a violent confrontation with law. Thanks to his betrayal of Governor O. Max Gardner, North Carolina authorities were determined to put Wood away for good, dead or alive. With so much attention from the press and police around the state, the bandit could no longer hide in plain sight, committing robberies in broad daylight. For Otto Wood, the deepening of the Depression meant a reckoning.

The Ford that Wood used for joyriding in December 1930 arrived with him from the Midwest, stolen from Heyes Motor Company in Claremore, Oklahoma. To make the car untraceable, Wood stole the license plate from a car registered in Joplin, Missouri.[2] Entering Virginia through Bristol, Otto and Celia Wood, along with her six-year-old daughter, Lucile, spent Christmas in southwestern Virginia, staying at points in and around Pulaski and Roanoke. Otto parted ways with Celia and her daughter sometime soon after Christmas and headed south toward North Carolina. Traveling through Rocky Mount, Virginia, Wood met Roy Banner Barker, a native of the coalfields near St. Paul, Virginia.[3] Barker had previously worked on the

farm of A. F. "Franz" Gray in Wilkes County and had been hitchhiking after
visiting the homes of family in Virginia for the holidays. Described as a
"fleshy fellow" by several people who met him while he accompanied Wood,
Barker seems to have been a loner for most of his life and probably was not
in the best of health. Though a young man—twenty-five years old at the time
he met Wood—Barker never found any steady employment and appears to
mostly have worked odd jobs as an itinerant laborer. A 1931 report stated
that Barker had previously served time for bootlegging, perhaps casting a
shadow of doubt on his later professed ignorance concerning Wood's identity and criminal activities.[4]

Wood and Barker made their way south into North Carolina, stopping
in Winston, where Wood bought Barker a shave in a barbershop and something to eat. Then, heading west, Wood again began a tour of his home
county, visiting relatives and stopping in on old neighbors. On the night of
December 29, the duo entered Wood's home community in the Antioch section of Wilkes, stopping at the house of Silas W. Johnson, a distant relative
whose kinship to Wood had been strengthened through bootlegging. Leaving Barker in the car, Wood walked into Johnson's house and—with a manner that can only be described as Robin Hood–esque—handed Johnson and
his children money. The four smallest children received pennies, and Silas
punched holes in them to make necklaces: good-luck charms. Wood then
gave Johnson's wife, Delia, a chicken and said that he would pay her five
dollars to cook it for the family's breakfast. Johnson remembered asking
Wood whether Barker knew who he was traveling with (referring to Wood's
status as a wanted man and outlaw). "Hell, no," Wood responded, "he don't
know who I am." When Johnson asked Wood if Barker would like to come
in out of the cold, Johnson recalled Wood said: "I don't care nothing about
him. He has an overcoat and some blankets. If they don't keep him warm,
let him freeze." Wood and Barker left the Johnson house in the early morning hours of December 30, never returning to eat the breakfast Wood "paid
for." Johnson noted that Otto flashed a roll of cash. He estimated that the
bandit had around "$200 or $300, perhaps more." Another of Wood's relatives, Eli Johnson, reported that the outlaw and his companion spent the
night nearby at the home of Eva Shew.[5]

At six in the morning on December 30, Wood and Barker emerged from
woods outside the home of J. H. Harris, not far away from the Johnsons'.
Telling Harris that their car was stuck in the mud, they sat down to eat
breakfast with Harris's family. W. L. Foster, another local man present at
the time of Wood's visit to the Harris home, remembered the outlaw trying
to haggle with Gordon Harris, JH's son, who was roughly the same age as

Wood, for an older-model pearl-handled .32/20 pistol. The elder Harris attempted to dissuade Wood from buying the gun, telling him that the rusty
pistol was broken and that "the children had been playing with it around
the yard." When Wood insisted that they make a deal, Gordon offered Wood
the gun for $2. Wood pulled $1.50 from his pocket, telling the younger Harris that was "all the money he had." Harris accepted the offer. Wood gave
the broken pistol to Barker.[6]

Continuing their tour of Wilkes County, the pair arrived that afternoon at
the store of Felix Staley. Once again leaving Barker in the car, Wood entered
the store in the company of several other men, buying cigarettes. Wood
visited with Staley and his wife in their home a short distance away before
leaving with Barker and the other men. When questioned by authorities
about Wood's visit, the storekeeper was unable—or perhaps unwilling—to
give names of those he saw accompanying the outlaw. Constable George
Holland encountered Wood and his entourage that evening. Wood stopped
Holland briefly, showing the constable a pistol and asking if he wanted a
drink of liquor. After Wood let him go, the constable made his way to a telephone but failed to reach Wilkes County sheriff William Somers. Holland
made his way into Wilkesboro the next morning, informing local officers
that Otto Wood was back in Dellaplane. The Wilkes County lawmen made
plans to corner Wood the next day.[7]

On New Year's Eve morning, Wood and Barker visited the cabin of "Franz"
Gray. Crippled by an accident several decades earlier, Gray had hired Barker
to help work his farm in early 1930. Otto talked with Gray while Barker left
to get yet another quart of whiskey. When Barker returned, Gray pulled him
aside. A report issued by Rowan County, North Carolina, authorities in January 1931 recorded the conversation as relayed by Gray himself:

> Gray said to Barker: Roy, I like Wood as a neighbor but I wouldn't be
> traveling around with him 'cause if he ever gets into a shooting scrape
> someone will get killed.
> Roy then replied that "he was not uneasy." . . .
> Gray then remarked: "you know he is an outlaw and has escaped
> from the penitentiary[?]" . . .
> To this, Roy replied: Uncle Franz, I am glad you told me about it. I
> know I ought not to be with him but it won't do to lay down on him now,
> because I am afraid of him. Besides, he promised to take me down to
> the eastern part of the state.[8]

Gray also told authorities that he was convinced that Barker had no idea of
Wood's identity until their conversation.[9] Leaving the Gray home at around

10:45 a.m., Barker reportedly called out to Franz Gray, "I'll be back tonight or in a few days." Gray described last seeing Barker climbing into Wood's car wearing an overcoat and carrying an unloaded pistol in his pocket.[10]

That afternoon, R. E. Ramsey of the Carolina Motor Club branch in Salisbury, Rowan County, North Carolina, became nervous as a man lingered too long in his shop. Operating a business selling license plates for cash only, Ramsey was likely already on high alert for potential robbers. When Ramsey asked the man if he wanted anything, the suspicious loiterer replied, "[I'm] waiting for a man," then left the shop after the span of only a few minutes. Ramsey would later confirm that Otto Wood had entered his shop, almost certainly casing it with an eye toward stealing cash.[11]

Ramsey was not the only one who noticed Wood's arrival in Salisbury. At around one o'clock in the afternoon, Chief of Police Robert Lee "RL" Rankin and Assistant Chief John W. Kesler received a tip that a man matching Wood's description had been seen downtown.[12] The tip was later revealed to have come from R. R. Cline, an ex-convict who knew Wood from the penitentiary. Cline ran into Wood and Barker on the street and ate lunch with them at a café before calling the police station.[13] Climbing into Rankin's car after their police vehicle failed to start, the two officers began a patrol of the city.[14]

Turning the corner from Lee Street onto East Innes Street, Rankin and Kesler spotted two men on the sidewalk, one with Wood's characteristic limp and left arm held firmly in a pocket.[15] Rankin pulled the car to the curb near the street corner. "Come here, buddy," Rankin called to Wood as he and Kesler stepped onto the wayside. "What do you want?" Wood responded. "Let me see your other hand," demanded the police chief, eliciting a round of cursing from Wood.[16] "Otto Wood, let me see your hand," Rankin ordered. "Here it is, dammit," Wood answered as he pulled a .45 Smith and Wesson from under his coat with his right hand.[17] "I'm Otto Wood and here is my hand," Wood boasted, his pistol covering Rankin and Kesler. "Move and I will kill you both."[18] Wood then motioned the officers back into the car, telling Roy Barker to get into the back seat. Otto jumped in behind Barker, leveling his pistol at Rankin in the driver's seat, and ordered the police chief to drive them out of town.[19]

R. L. Rankin had no intention of driving Wood out of town. Both he and Kesler were veterans of several gunfights with regional criminals; Rankin bore scars from a stomach wound received in one such encounter.[20] Already planning to engage the outlaw, the police chief pretended to struggle with the car's gears, deliberately keeping the car stopped, while asking "which way [Wood] wanted to go."[21] As Wood told the officers to drive him to the

Site of Wood's shootout with Rankin and Kesler, East Innes Street, Salisbury,
North Carolina. *Master Detective* magazine, 1933. (Author's collection)

train station, Rankin flung open the driver's side door and rolled out of
the car into the street, drawing his pistol as he scrambled for cover behind
the car's radiator.[22] Wood immediately followed, leaping out of the car and
firing wildly toward Rankin's position. Kesler and Barker left the car after
Wood, Kesler bringing his pistol into action against the outlaw.[23] Kesler's
position was near the back of the car on the passenger's side nearest to
Wood. One witness recalled Kesler firing from the back seat, but the officer
probably exited the car to join the fight—the witness likely saw Kesler near
the rear door using it as cover. Another contemporary account places Kesler within three or four feet of Wood when he opened fire.[24] Knowing that
Barker's pistol was inoperable, Wood called to his companion to pull his
gun, perhaps hoping to draw Kesler's fire away from himself. Barker made
no motion to help Wood.[25] An account published shortly after the gun battle
stated that once bullets started flying, Barker quickly hunkered down in the
car's back seat and called to Kesler: "Don't shoot me, I won't shoot you."[26]

The battle between Wood and the officers continued with shots fired over
the hood of Rankin's car. In the exchange of bullets, pieces of flying glass
from the car's windshield ricocheted across Rankin's face, leaving a series
of cuts. The police chief also received a scalp wound, probably a graze from
one of Otto's bullets.[27] As a shot from Kesler's pistol shattered one of Wood's
knees, Rankin and Wood exchanged one last salvo.[28] Rankin later recalled
the deadly moment: "I raised up from behind the radiator. I wanted to end
it. As I raised up I fired. Otto fired. We both shot at the same time. Otto
missed. My bullet went home."[29] Rankin's bullet passed through the side of
Wood's mouth and exited in gruesome fashion at an angle through the top
of the bandit's head.[30] Using Rankin's reminisces, the postscript of Wood's

Life History described the scene: "The shot which killed [Wood] hit him near the mouth, and tore a shattering wound through the side of his head. When the fatal bullet ploughed into Otto's head, he staggered and fell in the street, almost against the curb, his gun, which was splattered with blood, falling from his hand as he fell. He was dead almost immediately in a great pool of blood, which lay on the street about his body."[31] In the entire brief gun battle, which took only a matter of seconds, eleven shots were fired between Wood and the officers. Rankin rapidly emptied his pistol of all five shots he had loaded; Kesler had fired two shots, and Wood returned fire with four (the bullet in his leg likely threw off any attempted aim).[32]

With Rankin's car riddled by bullet holes and Wood's body bleeding out on the curb, people on the Salisbury street corner entered a state of shock. Rock Hill, South Carolina, native H. B. Powell, after witnessing the gunfight, found himself drafted as a stretcher-bearer carrying Wood's body to an ambulance.[33] Signing Wood's death certificate several days later, the coroner of Rowan County, Walter L. Tatum, listed Wood's trade as "Escaped Prisoner." After noting Wood's death as instantaneous from a "shot-wound by policeman," the coroner placed the word "outlaw" under "contributory causes."[34]

Confiscating the car Wood and Barker used to travel to Salisbury, police discovered a loaded rifle and two pints of bootleg whiskey.[35] Tracing the car's origins back to a garage in Claremore, Oklahoma, the Salisbury Chamber of Commerce sent a tongue-in-cheek telegram to Claremore-born humorist Will Rogers, asking whether the automobile was his. No answer from Rogers was ever recorded.[36] Placing Roy Banner Barker under arrest, Rowan County officials immediately began checking the story of Wood's companion. Prosecuting attorney J. Allan Dunn and Rowan County sheriff W. Locke McKenzie traveled to Wilkes County to conduct interviews with those residents who knew of Wood and Barker's movements in the days prior to the shootout. One of those interviewed, A. F. "Franz" Gray, told the officers that Wood was "a good hearted fellow but if you had $10 and Otto wanted it he would kill you to get it, if it was not given to him." Gray also told Dunn and McKenzie that his nephew, Ozie Gray, heard Wood say, "I'll make 'em earn their reward" when asked about the price on his head.[37] Determining from Dunn and McKenzie's report that Barker was only an acquaintance of Wood and not an accomplice, the Rowan County court sentenced him to a six months on a road gang for carrying a concealed firearm.[38] Governor Gardner offered Barker parole a month later on February 25, 1931.[39] After his parole, Barker largely disappears from the public record.

Celia Byrd Wood, the supposed bride and traveling companion of Otto Wood, sent a telegram home to her parents in High Point, North Carolina, asking for confirmation of her lover's death. The reply read: "O. H. Wood dead. Come home. We want you." Celia and her daughter returned home, arriving by train from Roanoke, Virginia, on January 2, 1931.[40] Reporters instantly set upon the mother and daughter, eager to get the scoop on their travels with Otto Wood. Although Celia mostly refused to talk, telling reporters "not to publish anything," she slipped in a few lines that showed her continued love for Otto and support of his outlaw ways. "Otto was a lot better than some of the folks who are calling him bad," Celia told the press. When asked if she were afraid of suspicions of her complicity in Wood's crimes, she stated firmly, "They [meaning the police] haven't got anything on me."[41] Three months later, Celia gave birth to twins, a boy and girl, and gave them the last name "Wood."[42]

Despite reports of the violent gunfight flooding the press, the events that occurred as his body lie unclaimed in a Salisbury morgue began to sway public opinion to a more sympathetic view of the bandit. Authorities in Salisbury sent a telegram to Governor Gardner asking for his advice on what should become of Wood's remains. Likely unwilling to have any further association with his failed experiment, Gardner never gave a response.[43] The undertaker caring for Wood's body hurriedly restructured the outlaw's mangled skull, placing the body on display the day after Wood's final gunfight. The mortician estimated that five thousand people visited G. W. Wright and Sons funeral home in downtown Salisbury to view Wood's body on New Year's Day alone.[44] As members of the public filed by Wood's corpse, Ellen Wood sent a telegram from Coaldale, West Virginia, to the Salisbury police headquarters: "I want to claim the body of Otto Wood. Will be there as soon as possible. Where is body located? Answer."[45] News of Ellen Wood's telegram circulated quickly. One Salisbury resident, hearing of Ellen Wood's message, sent a wreath of flowers to the funeral home. Attached to the bier holding Otto Wood's body, the wreath bore an inscription that read, "From a Mother to a Mother."[46]

On January 3, Luther Wood and Claude Blizzard, a brother-in-law of the Wood family, arrived in Salisbury in hopes of claiming Otto's remains.[47] Stopping at the police station, the men came face-to-face with Police Chief Rankin. Instead of a confrontation, the conversation between Luther Wood and Rankin was cordial, with Wood's older brother expressing relief that "Otto did not kill any one [sic] in his last encounter with the law." When he asked whether Rankin had found any personal effects on Otto's body, the police chief informed them he had found nothing but a .45 caliber pistol. "I'm frank to tell to you I want to pass that gun on to my descendants," Rankin said. Luther offered a good-natured a response, replying, "I can't say *I* blame you a bit." As the conversation turned toward the claiming of Otto's body, Wood and Blizzard found they were short of funds. As the *Statesville Landmark* reported: "[Wood and Blizzard] said they did not have the money to ship the body to West Virginia, have it buried and pay other expenses, yet they did not want the body sent to a medical school, or buried in the potter's field. They had some slight fear, also, that should the body be given a respectable burial [in Salisbury], some persons with ghoulish inclinations because of the widespread publicity given the shooting of the noted criminal, might be tempted to steal away the body."[48] Luther took Rankin into his confidence, telling him "he had spent several thousand dollars in helping his brother in recent years and had no more money to spend on his body." Wood and Blizzard left for Winston-Salem that afternoon to meet with James Wood and decide how to raise funds for their younger brother's remains. Perhaps in an effort to jumpstart fundraising efforts before leaving town, the men stooped to engage with one person of "ghoulish inclinations," selling the bloodstained suit worn by Otto during his final gunfight to the operator of a carnival.[49]

Adding to the Wood family's stress, a report circulated that Duke University had offered $50 to transport the outlaw's body to Durham for use in the medical school—a practice not unknown for the unclaimed bodies of convicts.[50] After a failed attempt to take out a loan to pay for Otto's burial, W. P. Byrd, the father of Celia Wood, stated that he "would have been satisfied if the body had gone to a pauper's grave rather than to a medical school."[51] Desperate to save face, a Duke representative called the Wright and Sons funeral home, telling the undertakers to inform residents that the story was not factual and that the medical school had made no such offer. While briefing the press of the university's statement, the undertakers told reporters that they had received multiple solicitations to purchase Wood's body for exhibition.[52]

The controversy surrounding Wood's body ultimately moved the people of Salisbury to action. Locals began a collection to provide for the costs of Otto Wood's final expenses. The effort raised $24.68 to ship the bandit's remains to West Virginia by express as well as an additional $39.44 to send to Ellen Wood for the burial. Rowan County citizens sent $15 for the purchase of a simple, silk-lined casket.[53] The Salvation Army and several private citizens reportedly provided Wood's body with "a blue serge suit, white shirt, dark necktie, and other accessories." On January 4, just four days after the bloody shootout in downtown Salisbury, hundreds of people gathered at the train station to see Wood's casket loaded on the afternoon train. The coffin was bedecked with floral wreaths and other decorations, including

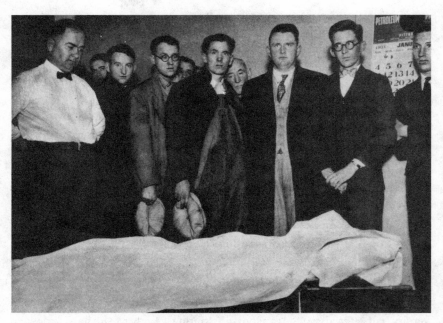

Wood's body photographed in the G. W. Wright and Sons funeral home, Salisbury, North Carolina. *Master Detective* magazine, 1933. (Author's collection)

one floral memorial purchased by local newsboys, who used some of their funds earned from newspapers detailing Wood's final moments.[54] In displaying kindness to the Wood family, Salisbury's citizens also took time to celebrate their own. The same week, the city council voted to award Rankin and Kesler gold medals acknowledging their bravery in confronting and killing Otto Wood.[55]

Initial reactions to the death of North Carolina's most noted criminal varied from author to author as various journalists and latter-day philosophers attempted to reveal their own truths about society as encapsulated and represented by the stories of the deceased outlaw. The details of Wood's death excited the press across the nation, with stories about Otto's life of crime featured in newspapers in far-flung places, from Green Bay, Wisconsin, to Honolulu, Hawaii.[56] The earthbound afterlife provided to Wood by these commentators balanced his image on a tightrope strung over the gulf between infamous sociopath and folk hero. Wood's hometown paper, the *Wilkes Journal-Patriot*, offered a brief eulogy that highlighted the events of Wood's life—Wood had "lived . . . longer than was expected," it said—and lauded him once again as the "Will o' the Wisp" of the North Carolina State

Prison in celebration of his "many and varied escapes."[57] A report published in the *Mount Airy News* offered a decidedly lengthy analysis of Wood's life and character. The column also addressed the conflicted opinions on Wood held by North Carolinians in the wake of his death:

> Every man who is not afraid to express his sentiments will admit that there is something about a daring man like Otto Wood that appeals to him. We all have admiration for the man who has no fear. With the passing of Mr. Wood there will be all kinds of reactions. Some will take him as a huge joke, a silly man who was able to treat a great state with impudence and laugh in the face of law and order. Others see him a man persecuted and justified in getting some kind of revenge for the ill treatment he received. Many will think of him as a victim of some kind of mental derangement and a man who should have been confined in the department for the insane.[58]

Following up on the charge of mental derangement, the Mount Airy writer speculated that Wood perhaps possessed a "defective brain," had perhaps "been spoiled in training," or "may have been both a victim of heredity and training." The columnist claimed that the fault for Wood's lifetime of crime grew from roots in either his education or the mistakes of "old Mother Nature." "The real sorrow," the *Mount Airy News* reporter lamented in a stern air of social commentary, "should be that any such condition should exist that makes possible an Otto Wood." The newsman ultimately proclaimed Wood "a misfortune and calamity for his day and generation . . . a freak, a man out of the ordinary and unable to make his life conform to the times in which he lived."[59]

"Mothers Will Need New 'Bogey Man,'" lamented the January 5, 1931, edition of the *Statesville Landmark*. The text explained the origins of an Otto Wood myth, a tale often told by Raleigh, North Carolina, mothers who warned that Otto "carried a big sack over his shoulder" to steal away spiteful children. During Wood's repeated escapes, the article recalled, this fanciful lecture on the evil Otto Wood enjoyed frequent use as a way to make children mind their elders.[60] A more serious column published in the same issue, titled "Thanks for the Removal of a Menace," portrayed Wood as a real-life monster and justified his death as "a desperate remedy for a desperate man." The author scolded officers of the law who "called too long with Otto Wood" and opined that the celebrated escape artist "had his chance, a far greater chance than he deserved," to redeem himself.[61] The Statesville writer further posited that Wood had playacted his way into the sympathies of the public and onto newspaper headlines:

Wood's career, his appeal to the spectacular, made him a sort of hero in the eyes of those to whom the dramatic appeals regardless of its content or the purpose of its content or the purpose of the play that produces the acting. To this glorification newspaper reporters who have made a business of playing up the fellow, made large contribution. By implication some seem to regret his death. . . . They are a-meanin' no harm but the harm that may be done by contributing to the dare devil plays of hardened criminals, murderers and potential murderers, is self-evident. Others will lament the "poor boy" that "never had a chance" and other stuff like that. [Wood] had all sorts of chances and proved himself unworthy of every opportunity for reformation.[62]

The article also reminded readers that the "duty of the government" and "all good citizens" must focus on "public protection" and deemed the death of men such as Wood necessary. "The law dallied long with Otto Wood in North Carolina," the reporter bemoaned, lauding the fact that "more lives were not sacrificed" before Wood's final shootout.[63]

In a passionate response to Wood's death, the *Mount Airy News* absolved Governor Gardner of any foolhardiness in his treatment of the deceased outlaw. "Governor Gardner was not hard to persuade," explained the report as its author reiterated how the "heart of the executive always beats double time for any fellow who is victim of the strength of the state." The newspaper stated that Gardner had "inherited" Wood from former governors Morrison and McLean and lauded the latter for his stand, which had placed the escape artist in solitary. Prisoners in the penitentiary, though they felt "regret that Mr. Wood had to die," reportedly held the "bitterest" sentiment against the bandit for his betrayal, which left them in "misery." The writer concluded that Wood's "treacherous treatment of Governor Gardner was a terrible blow to the welfare of every man and woman in the service of the state."[64] Although Wood's betrayal had exposed flaws in Gardner's push for a prison system intent on rehabilitation, the governor's overhaul of the Central Prison at Raleigh eventually succeeded. By February 1931, officials at the prison reported their population as "gaining at [a] fast rate." After receiving a record twenty-five prisoners in a single day, Governor Gardner and prison officials pressed for the building a new prison plant.[65] The result yielded the construction of over thirty camps by the end of 1931, which removed prisoners from the overcrowded cells in Raleigh. The sanitary conditions at these camps, though a marked improvement over Central Prison, were complicated by the lack of statewide funding and constituted, at best, a flawed victory for Gardner by the time he left office in 1933.[66]

During the months that preceded the shootout in Salisbury, Wood's popularity had waned. His failure as political pawn under the control of Governor Gardner, coupled with the onset of the Depression, translated his previous persona of a romanticized highwayman to that of a mentally deranged, dangerous vigilante who victimized innocent people. Yet despite the negative press prior to Wood's death, the spectacle produced by his last stand once again reshaped the bad man's image. The New Year's Eve gunfight yielded a Wild West–style conclusion to a lifelong crime spree and, in the months that followed, elevated Otto Wood to the status of a mythicized folk hero. The retrospectives on Wood's life published in newspapers inspired lyrical tributes from several southern balladeers, recording artists in a budding genre marketed as "hillbilly" music. The lyrical efforts of these pioneering country musicians chronicled Wood's exploits and celebrated him as a roguish yet sympathetic character. As the remains of Otto Wood, the man, were laid to rest on a hillside in southern West Virginia, the legendary "Otto Wood the Bandit" emerged, a latter-day answer to Robin Hood and Jesse James.

CHAPTER 8

STEP UP, BUDDIES, AND LISTEN TO MY SONG

THE BALLADS OF OTTO WOOD,

1931–PRESENT

Lythe and listen, gentilmen,
That be of frebore blode;
I shall you tel of a gode yeman,
His name was Robyn Hood.
—*The Gest of Robyn Hood*, ca. 1400

Step up, buddies, and listen to my song,
I'll sing it to you right but you might sing it wrong,
It's all about a man named Otto Wood,
I can't tell you all, but I wish I could.
—"Otto Wood, the Bandit," by Walter "Kid" Smith
   and the Carolina Buddies, Columbia Records,
   151345-2 (Co. 15652-D), February 24, 1931

O N TUESDAY, February 24, 1931, Walter Smith stood behind a microphone at Columbia Studios in New York City preparing to record a new selection of "hillbilly" songs. After the early success of the recordings of Fiddlin' John Carson in the mid-1920s, artists and repertoire (A&R) men from burgeoning labels such as Columbia and Victor had traversed through mill towns and railroad hubs south of the Mason-Dixon Line in search of singers and musicians, practitioners of what would become a new genre: country music. Auditions held in urban centers, such as Victor A&R man Ralph Peer's notable Bristol Sessions, attracted a stream of working-class hopefuls keen on both recording their songs and collecting at least some small profit from the hillbilly music craze. Farmers such as the Carter Family, a tuberculosis-plagued railroad brakeman named Jimmie Rodgers, and a former freight-hauling wagoner dubbed "Uncle Dave" Macon all gained popularity as they established themselves among the first professional stars of country music.

A native of Carroll County, Virginia, Walter "Kid" Smith was yet another such character in the cast of homegrown musicians who figured into the infancy of the country genre. Smith began his singing career in the musical culture surrounding the textile mills of Spray, North Carolina. A former sawyer and mill hand, he first earned his nickname, "Kid," in the boxing ring.[1] By the late 1920s, inspired by neighbors such as the popular banjoist and singer Charlie Poole, Smith had altogether ditched his earlier occupations for a career as a singer and composer of songs. Backed by guitarist Norman Woodlief and fiddler Odell Smith (a veteran of Poole's band), performing as the Carolina Buddies, "Kid" prepared for his February 1931 session a composition tailor-made for the ears of his neighbors in the foothills of North Carolina and Virginia.[2] Kid's song full of action, dialogue, and tragedy was a surefire hit that ripped inspiration from recent newspaper headlines. While Smith sang into the microphone, a nearby machine spun and whirred as a needle cut small ridges into a wax disc, chiseling out a 78 rpm memorial to the life and death of "Otto Wood, the Bandit."

With the burial of the body of notorious bad man Otto Wood near his mother's home in the hills of West Virginia, the spirit of Otto Wood the folk hero emerged. "Otto Wood Is Here!" shouted an advertisement in the *Burlington Daily Times* inviting "Every Citizen in This Community" to the Alamance Hotel for a "Sensational Prison Show."[3] The hotel lobby featured a free display of "Life-Like" wax dummies, the most prominent among them a likeness of the recently deceased one-handed bandit.[4] The exhibition apparently enjoyed some popularity with the public and continued through the fall of 1932. Wood's dummy stood within "a complete line up of all criminals of any national notoriety" that began with "Jesse James and his gang" and concluded with "Harry Powers (American Blue Beard)" alongside "Scarface Al Capone."[5]

Following on the heels of this traveling exhibition, Greensboro newspaperman C. R. Sumner announced his intention to publish his version of the story of Otto Wood, titled "Capturing the One-Handed Terror of the South." The *Lexington Dispatch* described Wood's life as one suitable to memoriam in a "detective story magazine": "The name and legend of Otto Wood, 'the one-handed terror of the South,' comes to the fore again, not with the violent emphasis of a few years ago, but with equally startling force from the pages of a detective story magazine which went on the stands last week. . . . It is a thrilling, absorbing piece that Sumner has woven about the misdeeds of the daring Otto Wood, whose amazing career rivaled that of Jesse James, Billy the Kid, and others famous in the outlaw history of this country."[6]

After a wealth of comparisons to Jesse James throughout his life, in death Wood took his place in the pantheon of uniquely American criminals.

In the days immediately after Wood's final gunfight, several amateur poets and balladeers submitted their works to North Carolina newspapers. One contributor, offering only the initials "OJ" as identification, sent a composition titled "A Ballad of Otto Wood" to the *Greensboro News*. Though not exactly the pinnacle of lyrical brilliance, the ballad offered a concise narrative of Wood's life and crimes:

Otto Wood he had one arm,
As a young man he had two;
But he got one cut off on the railroad
As brakeman will oftimes do.

[Chorus]
Otto he came from Wilkes county,
He loved women, song and wine;
He shot it out with Chief Rankin
And he died to a bullet's whine.

One hand was enough for the pistol
Which he always toted around,
A quick trigger finger had Otto,
As Kaplan at Greensboro found . . .

They tried and found him guilty,
Of murder in the second degree,
Gave him twenty-odd years to thirty
At Raleigh in the penitentiaree [*sic*].

But the prison could not hold him,
Four times he left Pou [prison superintendent George Ross Pou] cold;
If he had not met Chief Rankin,
He might have lived till he was old

Otto's brother's widow left her home
And children some three or four
And went with Otto away out west,
But she won't go there no more.

Otto met Rankin on a Salisbury street;
Says Rankin, "Where is your other hand?"

"This here one's enough," says Otto,
"To point your way to the Promised Land."

Chief Rankin he got in the auto,
Made out he was shifting the gear,
But grabbed instead for his pistol
And tumbled outside on [*sic*] his car.

When he got up he was shooting
And he fired through the windshield at Wood;
Some shots went wrong but it wasn't long
Till one of them did some good.

So Otto he died with his boots on,
With a hole in the side of his head;
The warden's prophecy was fulfilled,
For he hadn't a solitary red.

A rather nice exit for Otto,
A sneak, a thug and a crook;
And we don't care if they loosen his hair
In formaldehyde over at Dook.

No copyright has been applied for on the above and all banjo-pickers
are invited to step right in and help themselves.[7]

This early ballad of Otto Wood, though rough-hewn and lyrically unmusical in its construction, was the only ballad to place Wood's origins within Wilkes County. The ballad also references the false rumor of Duke University's ("Dook") offer on Wood's body, positing that the university wanted to perform phrenological experiments on the remnants of Wood's brain. The ballad also makes the erroneous assertion that Celia Byrd Wood, Wood's paramour and the widow of his younger brother, had "three or four" children at the time of their elopement in July 1930. Albeit uneven in verse and narrative—no "banjo-pickers" appear to have stepped forward to record the lyrics—the ballad appears to constitute the premier ballad-form memorial to Otto Wood.

Another example of a tribute to Otto Wood in a ballad form of rhyming sestets, or six-line stanzas, submitted to the Lumberton, North Carolina, paper, *The Robesonian*, was simply titled "Otto Wood." More a poem than a true ballad, the text bypassed all details of Wood's crimes to offer a brief overview of the writer's opinion of Wood's life and legacy:

Had Otto Wood
Lived as he should
He might have died unknown;
But he was ever
An artist clever
At breaking jails alone.

A life he saw
Of breaking law
And was his great renown;
Was ever sought
Until he fought
Police in Salisbury town

Whene'er he chose
From thence he rose
To show 'em he could;
Outlawed he fled
But for lead—
He'd still live as Otto would.[8]

Rife with jaggedly connected rhymes and puns, the poem stood as one of the most strained of the literary and musical creations produced about the bandit. Nonetheless, the text reveals the mixed feelings North Carolinians had on hearing of Otto Wood's violent end.

The first musicians to give a shellacked tribute to North Carolina's most famous outlaw were Bob Cranford and A. P. Thompson, a Tar Heel duo popularly associated with a string band known as the Red Fox Chasers. Hailing from Alleghany County, North Carolina, just northwest of Wood's home county of Wilkes, Cranford and Thompson likely knew of Otto Wood's exploits from local newspapers. In a recording session for Gennett Record's subsidiary Champion label held at Richmond, Indiana, on January 27, 1931—less than a month after the bandit's death—the pair waxed a guitar and harmonica duet with harmony vocals that eulogized the life and times of Otto Wood.[9] Set to a tune easily recognizable as the traditional ballad of "Jesse James," Cranford and Thompson's harmonies delivered a story that followed Wood's story from the slaying of Kaplan to his last moments in the shootout on the streets of Salisbury. The ballad's opening line even imitated the older lyrics about Jesse James and replaced "Jesse James, we understand, has killed many a man" with "Otto Wood, we are told, was mighty brave and bold." Despite the time limitations set by the recording technology of the era, the Carolina musicians managed to fit plenty of narrative detail into their short ballad that clocked in at just under three minutes long. The story-song repeated Wood's own tale of the loss of his hand in a railroad accident, a story he often told to the press, and loosely paraphrased Rankin's words spoken before the first shots of the outlaw's last gun battle. Though the song predominantly held to the facts as told by newspapers, the composition displayed some hints of sympathy toward the latter-day highwayman. "He was known throughout the land, for he had one only hand," one verse noted, then flaunted how the bandit nonetheless "in bravery traveled on his merry way."[10] In a slight contrast, the flip side of Cranford and Thompson's "Otto Wood" featured a cover of "Kid" Smith's song about Charlie Lawson, a Stokes County farmer who made headlines for the murder of his family on Christmas Day 1929.[11] The disc, which paired two bloody accounts of crime, sold well and became the most financially successful of the Otto Wood ballads:

Otto Wood, we are told,
Was mighty brave and bold
Who once was a brakeman on a train
But in a wreck one day
He lost his hand they say
And we feel so sorry for a man in pain.

In a North Carolina town
He shot a merchant down
And swung onto a car a-passing by
They went at his command
Outside the city limit
Then he put the driver out and passed him by

He was captured after awhile
And had to face his trial
To hear what the judge would have to say
His friends could do no good to help poor Otto Wood
"22 to 30 years you'll have to pay"

In about a half a year
Obtained a gun, we hear,
And forced a guard to drive him from the pen
But succeeded not, they say,

To make his getaway
But was captured and delivered back again

But they could not keep him there
Such confinement would not bear
He escaped from prison several times, they say,
He was known throughout the land
For he had only one hand
But in bravery journeyed on his merry way

He was in a town one day
Walking on his way
When he heard a man say "Buddy, come to me."
R. L. Rankin was the man
A hero brave and grand
Then Otto dared him move or death would be

Then their guns began to roar
Through his windshield bullets tore
Eleven from revolvers, it is said,
And the last from Rankin went
Into Otto it was sent
Then the news was heard that "Otto Wood is dead."[12]

Following on the heels of Cranford and Thompson's recording, Walter "Kid" Smith, another North Carolina musician eager to cash in on Wood's story, traveled to New York City to pitch his own composition titled "Otto Wood, the Bandit" to the Victor recording label.[13] Smith's "Otto Wood," much like Cranford and Thompson's, also made use of a more traditional melody, in this instance a fiddle tune known as "The Little Methodist."[14] "Kid" and his band, the Carolina Buddies, first auditioned the song for the Victor company, but after being rejected there they took the song to Columbia.

Arranged by fellow mill town musician Posey Rorer, a fiddler known by Columbia for his work with Charlie Poole and the North Carolina Ramblers, the February 25, 1931, recording session assured that Smith's record would reach the public while the memory of Wood's death still lingered vividly in their consciousness.[15] When Smith and the Carolina Buddies returned from New York, the Wilkes Journal-Patriot recognized their recording with the headline "Otto Wood to Achieve Immortality in Verse."[16] The Journal-Patriot column announced that, though "shot and killed," Wood "is to live

"Otto Wood," the mannequin, featured in a traveling "Crime Museum."
Photograph taken by Jack Delano, Farm Security Administration, in Henderson
County, North Carolina, March 1941. (Courtesy of the Library of Congress)

within the realm of 'canned music'" and offered a brief description of the recording trip: "Walter Smith, Norman Woodlief, and Odell Smith, a singing trio from Leaksville, N. C., passed through here today on their way home after having visited New York where they made a record of their new song, 'Otto Wood, the Bandit,' for a well known recording company. The ballad is one detailing the life of Otto Wood ever since he came into the public eye."[17]

Smith's "Otto Wood, the Bandit," accompanied by a catchy, syncopated guitar and fiddle duet, possessed the sound of a lighthearted romp that empathized with Wood and recounted his adventures. "Otto, why didn't you run / When the sheriff pulled out his .44 gun?" begged the song's chorus, alluding to the gunplay at Salisbury. With a bit of artistic license underlined by the reference to Chief of Police Rankin as "the sheriff," with his .38 police issue revolver recast as a ".44 gun," the song once again aligned Wood with the imagery of the Old West. The lyrics claimed that "he loved the women and he hated the law and he just wouldn't take nobody's jaw," an accentuation of Wood's rough, roustabout personality:

Step up, buddies, and listen to my song,
I'll sing it to you right but you might sing it wrong
It's all about a man named Otto Wood,
I can't tell you all, but I wish I could.

He walked in a pawnshop, a rainy day,
And with a clerk he had a quarrel they say,
He pulled out his gun and he struck him a blow,
And this is the way story goes.

They spread the news as fast as they could,
The sheriff served a warrant on Otto Wood,
The jury said murder in the second degree,
Then the judge passed the sentence to the penitentiary.

[Chorus]
Otto, why didn't you run?
Otto's done dead and gone
Otto Wood, why didn't you run
When the sheriff pulled out his .44 gun?

They put him in the pen but it done no good
It wouldn't hold a man they call Otto Wood
It wadn't very long til he slipped outside
Brought the gun on the guard, says, "Take me for a ride . . . "

Second time they caught him was a way out west
In a holdup game he got shot through the breast
They brought him back and when he got well
They locked him down in a dungeon cell

He was a man that they could not run
He always carried a .44 gun
He loved the women and he hated the law
And just wouldn't take nobody's jaw
[Chorus]

He rambled out west and he rambled all around
He met two sheriffs in a southern town
And the sheriff says, "Otto, step to the way
'Cause I been expecting you every day."

He pulled out his gun and then he said
"If you make a crooked move you'll both fall dead

Crank up your car and take me out of town . . . "
And a few minutes later he was graveyard bound.
[Chorus][18]

More original and poignant than Cranford and Thompson's take on the noted outlaw, the chorus of Smith's composition asked a question about Otto Wood's character that many North Carolinians had no doubt pondered since the Salisbury gunfight: Why hadn't Wood run? Why would an outlaw known for a lifetime of escapes and flights suddenly engage in battle with police? The previous violence exhibited by Wood seemed only a means to hinder those on his trail and, when finally cornered by lawmen, he always surrendered without a fight. Underneath a bouncy melody, Smith's prose pleaded to know what changed Wood and caused him to return fire at Salisbury. The unanswered question cast the Salisbury gunfight as a minor tragedy, a hindrance in the public's ability to understand a personality who possessed all the hallmarks of a folk hero. Smith later explained that in an interview that "he had rather strong feelings of sympathy for Wood."[19] Only two years younger than Wood, Smith probably saw an alternative version of himself in the outlaw.

Among those attracted by Walter "Kid" Smith's ode to "Otto Wood, the Bandit" was Bernard "Slim" Smith, a locksmith and inventor-turned–hillbilly songster from northern Mississippi. More talented as an entrepreneur than a songwriter, "Slim" Smith by 1931 had claimed a history of modest success in the music business with such compositions as the "Farm Relief Song," a topical piece on the plight of southern farmers recorded multiple times by the popular singer Vernon Dalhart.[20] "Slim" likely stumbled on "Kid" Smith's "Otto Wood" by happenstance in a visit to Victor Studios during the Carolina musician's audition. "Kid" Smith, in an interview with historian Norm Cohen, remembered someone taking notes during his audition of "Otto Wood, the Bandit." Music historian (and Charlie Poole relative) Kinney Rorrer later surmised that "the 'note taker' may have been Bernard Smith."[21] The almost exact copy of "Kid" Smith's line "he loved the women and he hated the law" makes a strong case that "Slim" Smith was person taking notes at the Carolina Buddies' audition. Lifting inspiration from "Kid" Smith's ballad, "Slim" Smith's composition was recorded twenty days before the Carolina Buddies' ballad and beat "Kid" Smith's version to the record shelves.[22]

Better acquainted with the sounds of urban vaudeville than "Kid" Smith and the Carolina Buddies, Bernard "Slim" Smith jazzed up the lament for the outlaw with a jumpy swing guitar rhythm and solos by Hawaiian steel guitarist "King" Benny Nawahi. The Appalachian ballad with a hula beat

Labels of Otto Wood ballads released on 78s.
(From the collection of Marshall Wyatt)

appeared in a March 1931 press release alongside other Victor releases, such as "Blue Yodel No. 8" by Jimmie Rodgers and "On the Rock Where Moses Stood" by the Carter Family.[23] Smith's vocals delivered a blend of lyrics from the two previous Otto Wood ballads as well as other lines probably inspired by newspaper accounts:

> Now listen, folks, while I sing this song,
> I'm tellin' the truth but it may sound wrong,
> It's all about poor Otto Wood,
> I'm sure he did everything he could,
> T'was in the pawnshop one rainy day,
> The truth may hurt but I must say,
>
> He struck his man with awful blows,
> And here's the way the story goes,
> They spread the news as fast as they could,
> The sheriff said, "People, catch Otto Wood!"
> "The murder, it's murder, the second degree,"
> And the judge sent Wood to the penitentiary.
>
> He was sent to the pen but it did no good,
> It wasn't strong enough to hold Otto Wood,
> He managed some way to get outside,
> And with his pistol he demanded a ride,
> And no one knows how he got his gun,
> But we do know that Otto won't run.
>
> They finally caught him a way out west,
> But had to shoot him in the chest,

They brought him back and got him well,
And locked him into a dungeon cell,
And there he stayed for days and days,
Until he promised he'd change his ways,

He was a man that would not run,
And he always carried his .44 gun,
He loved the women and hated the law,
And just wouldn't take nobody's jaw,
He thought he was an awful bet,
But now he leaves a story that's sad,

And here's the way the story goes,
They spread the news as fast as they could,
The sheriff said, "People, catch Otto Wood!"
"It's murder, it's murder in the first degree!"
And they sent poor Wood to the penitentiary,

He rambled out west and all around,
And when he came back to the southern town,
He was met by Rankin and Kesler, they say,
And there he had everything his way,
He defended himself the very best he could,
But the law laid claim for Otto Wood.[24]

"Slim" Smith's verses repeatedly used the words "awful" and "poor" as descriptive of Otto Wood and his acts. Even the darker stories of Wood's life, the murder of Kaplan included, Bernard Smith cast as "awful," unfortunate events that happened to Wood rather than having been caused directly by him. "Poor" Otto Wood, the victim, suffered through his life, a rebel who tried to live by his own terms. These terms put him at odds with the state and led to his martyrdom at Salisbury. The song echoed the *Mount Airy News*'s assessment of Wood as "a man out of the ordinary" and "unable to make his life conform to the times in which he lived."[25] By Smith's account, Otto Wood, an Old West character in the automobile age, was cornered by forces beyond his control. His death, though lamentable, constituted a necessity in order for society to progress. With characters like Wood relegated to the rogue's gallery of the past, with society cleansed, the reform movement that previously experimented with Otto Wood could march on without impediment. "Slim" Smith's composition pointed to the gray area where neither Otto Wood nor the state adequately represented the villain.

In the true spirit of ballad tradition, Wood left "a story that's sad," a violent warning for the benefit of all those who heard the verses.

A year later, another Otto Wood ballad by North Carolina textile worker and songsmith Dorsey Dixon appeared on April 28, 1932, in the *Rockingham Post-Dispatch*. Dixon's song, titled "The Shooting of Otto Wood," lifted language from earlier ballads—most notably the last verse, which parallels the 1912 ballad of Virginia outlaw Claude Allen, to summarize Wood's final days:

Just a fatal story of Otto Wood,
A wayward boy was he
The master and king of prison bars
Was bound on getting free
But one sad night he met his fate
He fell like many more
'Twas when he blowed into Salisbury
Played out and feeling sore.

A wise guy told chief Rankin
That Otto had blowed in town
The assistant chief was summoned out
They began to beat around
And when they ran into him,
Well, it was a finished fight
With law and order for their aim
And Otto for his life.

Chief Rankin then gave his command
For him to show his hand
We have a warrant for Otto Wood
We are out to get our man
Here's my hand, he grumbled
As he pulled a forty-five
The next cop that arrests me
Will not get me alive.

Yes, my name is Otto Wood
I've traveled miles around
I did not mean to disturb your peace
When I blowed in your town
It seems you're looking for trouble

Well, that is my middlename [*sic*]
If you're not looking for trouble, Chief,
Just take me to the train.

The Chief says, Otto, we've got you, boy,
And you may as well give up
But the roar of a forty-five was heard
And men began to duck
For Otto's gun had blazed away
To seal Chief Rankin's fate
But he ducked down and Otto found
He had flashed his gun too late.

The roar of guns was raging loud
As the officers answer[ed] fire
It was a terrible excited crowd
That was near the outlaw's car
Alas, Chief Rankin's only ball
A savage forty-five
He knew that he must make it count
For Otto was alive.

He raised up there before the car
With the ball that he had left
It was a narrow chance to take
He faced the jaws of death
The roar of guns had died away
Two men with nerves of steel
Faced each other standing there
Through broken car windshield.

That awful roar was heard again
When both their guns were flashed
Otto reeled and staggered back
He knew his check was cashed
Two men in a dazed when guns blazed
And a melting ball of lead
Whizzed and crashed its deadly way
Through the bold bad outlaw's head.

A coroner's inquest then was held
And a verdict soon was found

That the law was justified
In shooting Otto down
It was a terrible battle
Raging there in the heart of town
And it was sad to stand and see
A dying man go down.

It was only the end of a wayward life
Just take this tip from me
Don't lead the life that Otto led
It's fatal, don't you see.
That night Salisbury
Was crowded out five thousand rich and poor
Come to see the bold bad man
In death forevermore.

Watch your step as you travel this life,
Don't make that great mistake,
And then cry out for mercy
And help for it may be too late,
Otto Wood is now peacefully sleeping
Beneath the cold, cold clay,
But, oh, the stand he must take
In that Resurrection Day![26]

With an added dose of spiritual reckoning, Dixon transported Wood's story to higher moral ground. Wood's fault lay not in "mental deficiencies" but in a deficiency of the spirit that held repercussions far beyond the grave. By resetting Wood's final gunfight to nighttime, the balladeer set the dark tone of moral retribution that pervades the song. A tragic figure, Otto Wood forsook the narrow path of Christian values for his own crooked path to destruction. Dixon's ballad echoed words written by Otto Wood himself: "There is only one road away from trouble and that is along the straight and narrow road. The other pathway may seem smooth sailing for awhile; but it cannot last."[27] By Dixon's account, no matter how heroic Wood may have seemed in life and lore, the outlaw's sins would plague him in the afterlife.

Although he had previously had a modestly successful recording career as "the Dixon Brothers" with his brother, Howard, Dixon's song seems to have never made it to the recording studio. With the economic downturn of the Great Depression, record labels cut their losses and sacrificed the niche markets of hillbilly and race records. "Kid" Smith's "Otto Wood, the

Bandit," released in April 1931, sold 2,713 discs, numbers termed "respect-able" by country music historian Kinney Rorrer, who acknowledged that "other records were selling by the hundreds by this time." "Slim" Smith's version, recorded and released earlier on March 27, 1931, outsold the Carolina Buddies' record, selling a total of 3,138 copies.[28]

Despite returns well short of hit records, the songs recorded by Cranford and Thompson, Walter "Kid" Smith, and Bernard "Slim" Smith, as well as the stanzas by Dorsey Dixon, were all were significant as examples of a shift in the tradition of ballad making. Their songs continued the practice of songsters who observed notable events contemporary to their own time and memorialized them in verse. As ballad scholar M. J. C. Hodgart explains, among the functions of balladry as passed down from the British Isles was the means to celebrate locality: "[Ballads] are about minor events in national history, which are, of course, major events for local community, some of which have been recorded in historical documents. There is no clear dividing line between these ballads and the properly historical. . . . They record heroic actions like cattle-raiding and bridestealing, murders, and intrigues."[29] The musicians who wrote and recorded their versions of Otto Wood ballads participated in this ancient, history-recording process, yet they functioned in a new environment created by national recording labels. Instead of the ballad sheets of the Old World, these musicians used the modern recording technology to preserve and disseminate their songs. "Although they were professional musicians," wrote musician and folklorist Patrick Sky, "the Carolina Buddies were steeped in the tradition of Southern ballads and songs, and the songs that they were likely to write would be traditional in flavor."[30] These pioneers of country music bridged the divide between the story-songs passed down in the foothills of the Southeast and the industrialized atmosphere created by the labels that spawned the country music genre.

Unfortunately for Otto Wood's legacy, the advancement of technology stifled the ballads from attaining the prominence of more traditional songs such as "Jesse James." "[Wood's] immortality was in the hands of traditional musicians operating within a popular culture format that had its seasonal popularity," wrote Patrick Sky, "and his reputation was soon buried by the next season's hits." Sky concluded that just as Wood "had the misfortune of being born generations later than Jesse James or Robin Hood," his reputation and longevity in contemporary memory suffered the same fate, as modernization removed the songs about him from the oral tradition and left them static in the form of records.[31]

Three decades after Otto Wood's death, North Carolina guitarist and singer Arthel "Doc" Watson revived Walter "Kid" Smith's "Otto Wood, the Bandit." Watson, who grew up in Watauga County, adjacent to Wilkes in western North Carolina, was a child when Wood died and likely heard the Carolina Buddies' ballad on their record near the time of its release. The interest in string band sounds brought on by the folk revival of the 1960s allowed Watson, who had previously played electric guitar in regional honkytonks and square dance halls, to make a living playing the traditional music learned in his childhood. In adding the "Kid" Smith ballad to his set list, Watson introduced Wood's story to audiences at colleges and folk clubs. Watson and his son, Merle, recorded their version of "Otto Wood the Bandit" on the appropriately titled 1965 album *Doc Watson and Son*.[32] Perhaps evidencing the influence of Watson's version, the Possum Hunters, a string band made up of students at the University of California, Los Angeles, recorded their version of the "Kid" Smith composition on the LP *Death on the Highway (and Other Southern Lullabies)* a year later. The album was released on noted American Primitive guitarist John Fahey's Takoma label.[33] County Records, a Virginia-based label focusing on old-time and bluegrass music, reissued the Carolina Buddies recording on the album *Old Time Ballads from the Southern Mountains (Recorded 1927–1931)* in 1972. "Kid" Smith's Otto Wood ballad appeared alongside other regional ballads about train wrecks, murders, and myriad other unfortunate events.[34]

While old-time and bluegrass artists continued to record "Otto Wood, the Bandit," story-songs about the outlaw also found an unlikely home in the repertoires of southern garage rock and post-punk music in the 1990s and early 2000s. In 1994, Memphis, Tennessee–based garage rock band '68 Comeback recorded a cover of "Kid" Smith's Otto Wood ballad on their album *Mr. Downchild*. Headed by "Monsieur Jeffrey Evans," the group gave the ballad a frenetic, barely hinged rockabilly beat, pulsing behind a loose rendering of Smith's original lyrics.[35] Though it is decidedly untraditional, the gritty feel of '68 Comeback's "Otto Wood" spiritually fit the intensity of the life Wood lived. The Chapel Hill–based alternative rock group Snatches of Pink recorded their song "Otto Wood" on the album *Hyena*. Written by bandleader and songwriter Michael Rank, the song never explicitly references Wood's life, but the reappearance of the name "Otto Wood" in the chorus and the lyrical roughness of the song suggest that the bandit served as at least some inspiration.[36] Contemporary folk songwriter Larry Shores, originally from western North Carolina, paid tribute to Wood's memory on his album *Songs of T-Town*. Shores's Otto Wood song compares Wood to Tom Dula, sympathetically casting the infamous Wilkes Countians as men "who never understood" how to abide the laws society placed on them.[37]

Program from the second season of *Otto Wood: The Bandit*, an
outdoor drama performed in the Record Park, North Wilkesboro,
North Carolina. (Courtesy of the *Wilkes Record*)

In part due to Doc Watson's continued performance of "Kid" Smith's Otto
Wood, public interest in Wood's story regenerated nearly three-quarters of
a century after the outlaw's death. *The Record*, a North Wilkesboro, North
Carolina, newspaper printed a series of articles on Wood throughout the
early 2000s and sold reprinted copies of Wood's *Life History*.[38] Among those
featured in the retrospectives on Wood's life was Thurmond Sparks, Wood's
second cousin, who recalled the Robin Hood–like qualities of his relative:
"My mamma told me a lot about him. . . . She said he wouldn't rob from a

poor person. I think he was a good man. He wasn't bad to fight. He didn't want to harm anybody. He just wanted to rob." Hubert Foster, another of Wood's cousins, remembered a similar story: "People loved to see him come. He was kind of like Santa Claus. Back then, times were tough. He'd bring people clothes, like shirts and overalls. They knew he had stole them from somewhere, but they didn't care."[39] The stories, while not entirely excusing Wood's criminal activities, acknowledged that the outlaw had intermittently shown charity to the people of Wilkes during his nationwide crime sprees.

In addition to the series in *The Record*, the Elkville String Band, a group of veteran Wilkes County musicians formed as part of the cast of the outdoor drama *Tom Dooley: A Wilkes County Legend*—which celebrated another local "bad man"—generated further regional enthusiasm for Otto Wood tales with their own recording of Walter "Kid" Smith's composition.[40] Spearheaded by *The Record*'s editor, Jerry Lankford, and publisher, Ken Welbourn, the community of North Wilkesboro dramatized Wood's exploits with their own outdoor drama, *Otto Wood: The Bandit*. The play, written by Lankford, featured a cast of local volunteers and drew audiences that included members of Wood's family as well as several elderly people familiar with Wood's story from their childhood.[41] The performance of Lankford's drama continued for five seasons, produced every summer from 2011 to 2015 in the Record Park in North Wilkesboro.[42]

The ballads written about Otto Wood, though initially subject to the economic downturn that tanked sales of early country records, ultimately shaped what little is known about the outlaw today. "Kid" Smith's composition, thanks in no small part to Doc Watson's cover, continues to inspire those who hear it to seek out the details surrounding Wood's story. Wood's legacy is curated through the song, popular in a small section of western North Carolina and within a niche community of folk music enthusiasts located around the world. Most importantly, the ballad of "Otto Wood, the Bandit" returned Otto Wood home. The song inspired the community in Wilkes County—whom he once blamed as the cause of his crimes—to embrace him as a semilegendary character, celebrating his charity alongside the exploits of his criminal activities. Otto Wood is now western North Carolina's latter-day Robin Hood, with musicians still repeating "Kid" Smith's poignant, sympathetic line "Otto, why didn't you run?"

OTTO, WHY DIDN'T YOU RUN?

Joseph Ritson, the stoop-shouldered scholar who gave years to research into the life, times, and works of Robin Hood, insists his hero's surname was in reality Wood. This, Ritson observes, might signify the wood of Robin's trusty bow, or the wood of Sherwood Forest, where he sheltered his merry men. If Ritson speaks truth, it is not impossible that another outlaw, who electrified North Carolina as lately as New Year's Eve of 1930, descended from Nottinghamshire's rugged individualist.

—Manly Wade Wellman, "Otto Wood Kept Law on the Jump,"
  Raleigh News and Observer, January 10, 1954

Speaking of getting tired, old, etc., as most of us are inclined to do as we move into another year, here is something that will make a lot of North Carolinians—especially those in the western counties—feel old. Otto Wood, the nearest thing North Carolina had to a Dillinger-type roustabout in the roaring '20s, never lived to see 1931 move on the scene. 25 years ago last Saturday . . . Otto Wood was killed in an old-fashioned gun battle.

—"FEELING OLD DEPT.," *Spring Hope (NC) Enterprise*,
  January 5, 1956

T HE LIGHTS FLICKER UP at the Record Park in North Wilkesboro. A silhouette limps into view, appearing from around the corner of the small stage. Local actor Nat Padgett has the look down—he holds his left hand firmly in the pocket as he lopes his way onto the gravel path illuminated by spotlights. "Otto? Is that you?" Another actor emerges in a police uniform leveling a pistol. "Jimmie? Is that you? . . . When'd you start being law?" Both actors smile, raising pistols then dropping the weapons to their sides, talking of family and home, quickly raising the pistols again anytime the other moves. The audience laughs. "You're not going to take me are you, Jimmie?" "Not today . . . " The spotlights start to dim as Padgett moves toward the back of the stage. "Jimmie! Do you see him?!" a voice calls from offstage. "Nope! He's long gone!" The lights flicker off. For residents of Wilkes County, Otto Wood is alive again.

When viewed within the context of primary sources, Otto Wood—the man and the myth—provides a study of a person and a persona created within a time of intense social change. Wood's life coincided with the beginning of the Progressive Era in the 1890s, reached its midpoint in the atmosphere of reform politics in the 1920s, and culminated during the Great Depression. Although Wood's motivation for his criminal activities was chiefly personal gain, he still reacted to and lived under the political and social environment that influenced Appalachians during his lifetime. The narrative arc of Wood's story is full of attention-grabbing exploits of car chases and gunplay, but behind the spectacle it offers subtle hints of experiences and issues encountered by Appalachians in the late nineteenth and early twentieth centuries. Wood's life constituted a historical cross section important to the foothills and mountains of Appalachia, the state of North Carolina, and the broader history of the southern United States.

The examination of Wood's earliest years in Wilkes County and the coalfields of West Virginia provides a glimpse into the culture of rural people in the late nineteenth-century South. Wood's childhood wanderlust and train-hopping may have been exceptional in degree, but his nomadic nature was by no means an anomaly. Movement for better occupational opportunities was a fact of life necessitated by the economic realities of the rural Appalachia in the early 1900s. The neglect that Wood reported as a key feature of his home life in Wilkes County prompted him to enter the cycle of traveling for better prospects early in his childhood and, through extended family connections, led him to the coalfields of southern West Virginia. The teenage years Wood spent in the rough environment of the preunionized coalfields exposed him to a lifestyle that focused on survival and profit by any means necessary. The economic conditions of this time and place, in addition to the physical limitations on employment caused by Wood's crippled hand and foot, placed the young man on a social fringe where this mindset of survive and profit was taken to the extreme. The introduction of rail systems and the automobile within Wood's lifetime also allowed for an increased mobility not previously available to people from his region. Wood used these modern forms of transportation throughout a lifetime of car thefts and train-hopping that extended across the United States.

Wood's rise into the public spotlight in the 1920s coincided with a trend of progressivism in the southern political climate. The outlaw's roots in the rural landscape of western North Carolina contrasted with the suave appearance noted by reporters who visited him at his cell in Greensboro after his arrest for the murder of A. W. Kaplan. The Otto Wood of 1923 and 1924 encapsulated an image of the dual nature of a South on the brink of social and economic reform—he was a common man from a humble background who became a public figure through his crimes. Was Wood was transformed in image from "the Outlaw of the Boone Trail" and a regional scourge in western North Carolina to a controversial individual of statewide and national importance, the reports on his criminal nature and the debates inspired by his actions revealed much about the society that critiqued him. In an era of prison reforms and disputes about capital punishment, Wood made his voice heard through written statements to newspapers and endeavored to establish himself as a victim of a corrupt and antiquated prison system.

At the height of his fame in the mid-1920s, Wood cashed in on his celebrity with the publication of his *Life History*. The language featured in the manuscript further attached him to reformist politics focused on the eradication of poverty and the uplift Appalachian and the wider South through education. Wood's escapes from 1925 to 1927 received extensive coverage in the press and framed the most intensive period in which the fugitive wrote directly to newspapers. Through his letters, from both the prison cell and hideaways up and down the spine of the Appalachians, Wood stated his case as a victim of poverty, neglect, and the cruel conditions of the penitentiary. Wood's carefully constructed pleas and attempts to bargain with both officials and the public cast a light on the issues of education, poverty, and crime within the outlaw's home region.

In the late 1920s, North Carolina governor O. Max Gardner recognized Wood's potential as a poster child for his reform-driven political platform that focused on the same issues that had hallmarked Wood's attempts to justify his criminal lifestyle. The infamous convict encapsulated everything that the governor wished to restructure within his state. Gardner picked Wood, North Carolina's most publicized criminal, to conduct "an experiment in humanity" so he could demonstrate his powers of social reform from the bottom up. Wood used Gardner's willingness to experiment to allow for his last flight from prison, a decision that polarized the public against displaying any further amusement at his crimes. The onset of the Great Depression during these final years caused the public to drop all tolerance for Wood's antics and prompted Carolinians to reconceive Wood as a dangerous outlaw.

Wood's death removed him as a perceived threat to society and allowed him, through hindsight, to attain the status of a folk legend. The deceased bandit came to embody an outcast, a remnant of an earlier time when

Cover art for *Master Detective* magazine, featuring C. R. Sumner's article "Capturing the One-Handed Terror of the South." (Author's collection)

western North Carolina was still a frontier. This image skewed the reality of Otto Wood's lifetime and ignored the modernization and industrialization that had produced the outlaw more than any remnant of a frontier past. Historian Eric Hobsbawm, in a study of outlawry throughout history, coined the term "social bandit" to name the criminal type personified by Wood. Hobsbawm contended that the "peasant bandit" represented a phenomenon that emerged whenever rural societies met industrialization—an environment in which criminals pitted the landscape against the newfound wealth and population of industry for personal gain.[1]

Through his memorialization in ballads, Otto Wood came to represent a merging of the past and the present. The man who had once been "The One-Handed Terror of the South" was, in death, a comforting connection to the past, a residual embodiment of the lawlessness of another era. The midwestern Depression-era desperados, such as Charles Nelson "Pretty Boy" Floyd and John Dillinger, shared some similarities with Wood—notably rural roots and perceived "Robin Hood" qualities—but these men are now largely remembered as criminals within a brief period of operation. They were part of a modern crime wave overlapping with, yet entirely separate from, the period occupied by Otto Wood. Wood inhabited the middle ground between such elder southern and western criminals as Jesse James and the more modern criminals who followed, and met a similar violent end, in the middle of America's Great Depression.

The story of Otto Wood sits comfortably among such dark yet rollicking tales as those of Dillinger and Floyd, a story ripe for film and fiction. Through performances of the ballad of "Otto Wood, the Bandit," Wood has now traveled more as a song than he ever did a person (and that is saying a lot)! Wood, portrayed as the generous rebel who, per "Kid" Smith's song, "loved the women and hated the law / And just wouldn't take nobody's jaw" is now part of Appalachia's contribution to the ballad tradition. Like any good ballad, Wood's story will always remain incomplete and attract new lines to give greater detail even though, as "Kid" Smith's ballad reminds us, "Otto's done dead and gone."

ACKNOWLEDGMENTS

FIRST AND FOREMOST, this book would not have been possible without Herb Key, whose shoeboxes full of Otto Wood files started the research for this project back in 2008. Herb's encouragement and enthusiasm for sharing all things Otto Wood drove me to further research on the outlaw's life. Descending like an Appalachian version of a fairy godmother was Dr. Sandy Ballard, who always reminded me: "Don't forget about Otto!" Her guidance made the telling of Wood's story possible, and she seemed to somehow always find time in a very busy schedule to help me with a new draft of a chapter or even just a line or phrase. Really, she is truly magical and an inspiration to me and a host of others. Dr. Bruce Stewart was the baking soda that made this volcano. Bruce made me realize that a book on Otto was possible, and his direction on how to write the proposal for this manuscript gave me shove I needed to get started. I admire and appreciate him as both a friend and a historian. Lucas Church at UNC Press has been a constant companion through the process of getting this book produced. I was tickled to work with someone with a passion for Appalachian stories and with the knowledge of how to present them to the world. I was thrilled to have David Holt write the foreword to this book. His work in preserving stories and music from this region, including those about Otto, made him the perfect person to kick this thing off.

On the research side of things, I must thank the W. L. Eury Appalachian Collection at Appalachian State University, which provided many of the rare local books and microfilms used as sources in this work. Thanks to Appalachian State Special Collections and Research Center for keeping me employed! Gregg Kimball, director of public services and outreach, and the staff of the Library of Virginia turned up prison records and a mugshot of a young Otto Wood that aided in the early portions of this book. Kevin Young educated me on the statutes of outlawry as they existed in North Carolina throughout history, which was invaluable to understanding the world Otto Wood lived in. Thanks to those at the West Virginia Department of Corrections, the Tennessee State Archives, the Ohio History Connection, the Wilkes Heritage Museum, and the Library of Congress. I also need to mention some others who have delved into tracing the Otto Wood story and helped make this book possible: Jerry Lankford and Ken Welborn at *The*

Record in North Wilkesboro, Marshall Wyatt (who provided the images of 78s), Kinney Rorrer, Patrick Sky, and Paul Coffey.

Thanks to my folks, Jim and Kim McKenzie, who encouraged my interest in history from an early age, an interest that started from the ground up on the farm where they raised me. Their love, support, and pride in work are things I carry with me always. Thank you to Steve Kruger, Dustin Witsman, and countless other friends who have checked in on how this book was going and hyped it up to others. Finally, I must acknowledge the love and companionship of Dr. Savannah Paige Murray, most certainly the best thing I ever found in a library. Her encyclopedic knowledge, wit, and support throughout this whole process made it a thousand times better. I look forward to many more years "further on down the road" of exploring cool places, playing and listening to music, and generally just having a good time.

OTTO WOOD TIMELINE

May 9, 1893	Commonly accepted date for Otto Wood's birth (listed by Wood himself on World War I draft card and by his family on tombstone)
August 1907	Sent to the Iredell County, North Carolina, chain gang for petty thefts
February 1909	Arrives at Stonewall Jackson Training School, a North Carolina reform school
April 29, 1911	Loses his left hand in a shotgun accident
March 27, 1913	Arrested for breaking into train cars at Graham, Virginia
May 10, 1913	Enters Virginia State Penitentiary
May 15, 1913	Escapes from Road Camp 27, Spotsylvania County, Virginia
September 7, 1913	Returns to Virginia State Penitentiary after capture in Wilkes County, North Carolina
November 20, 1914	Second escape from Road Camp 27, Spotsylvania, Virginia
November 13, 1915	Arrested for car theft after chase in Salisbury, North Carolina
November 1915	Breaks from Iredell County, North Carolina, chain gang shortly after trial
September 1916	Declared outlaw by Wilkes Superior Court after multiple car thefts
October 1916	Captured in Chattanooga, Tennessee
December 3, 1916	Arrives at Tennessee Penitentiary
May 28, 1917	Breaks out of Tennessee Penitentiary
June 2, 1917	Captured in Wilkes County, North Carolina
June 8, 1917	Returned to Tennessee Penitentiary
April 27, 1918	Second break from Tennessee Penitentiary
September 5, 1918	Arrives at West Virginia State Penitentiary after being captured and sentenced for car theft in McDowell County
January 9, 1919	Escapes from West Virginia State Penitentiary alongside James Borders
January 30, 1919	Wood's younger brother and partner in crime, Robert, dies of Spanish flu

May 16, 1919	Captured in Wilkes County, North Carolina
May 20, 1919	Returned to West Virginia State Penitentiary
January 17, 1920	Returned to Tennessee Penitentiary after mass pardons in West Virginia
February 16, 1921	Third and final escape from Tennessee Penitentiary
August–September 1921	Operates as a highwayman under the alias "Jennings" in Texas
September 23, 1921	Captured in a stolen car in Portsmouth, Ohio
November 1921	Sent to Ohio State Penitentiary, booked under the alias "Charles Jones"
June 21, 1923	Escapes from road gang in Ohio
September 1923	Operates as a highwayman in Kentucky and Tennessee under the alias "Jack Boggs"
November 3, 1923	Kills Abraham W. Kaplan, a Greensboro, North Carolina, pawnbroker
November 10, 1923	Captured in Mercer County, West Virginia, returned to Guilford County, North Carolina
December 1923	Convicted of second-degree murder and sent to North Carolina State Prison
May 10, 1924	Escapes from North Carolina State Prison with John Starnes
May 12, 1924	Wood and Starnes captured in Roanoke, Virginia, and returned to North Carolina State Prison
November 23, 1925	Second escape from North Carolina State Prison
December 7, 1925	Captured in Iredell County, North Carolina and returned to North Carolina State Prison
July 1926	*Life History of Otto Wood* published
November 22, 1926	Third escape from North Carolina State Prison
January 25, 1927	Shot and captured in Terre Haute, Indiana
February 18, 1927	Returned to North Carolina State Prison, sent to death row for solitary confinement
July 1929	Released from death row
May 20, 1930	Made "A Grade Prisoner" by North Carolina State Prison officials
July 10, 1930	Fourth and final escape from North Carolina State Prison
December 31, 1930	Killed in shootout on the streets of Salisbury, North Carolina

NOTES

ABBREVIATIONS

ACT	Asheville Citizen-Times	NWR	The Record (North Wilkesboro, NC)
AS	Anniston (AL) Star	OMI	Messenger-Inquirer (Owensboro, KY)
BDT	Burlington Daily Times	PDT	Portsmouth Daily Times (Portsmouth, OH)
CO	Charlotte Observer	RHH	Rock Hill (SC) Herald
CVN	Clinch Valley News	RNO	Raleigh News and Observer
DB	The Bee (Danville, VA)	RTD	Richmond Times-Dispatch
GDG	Gastonia Daily Gazette	SEP	Salisbury Evening Post
GDN	Greensboro Daily News	SP	Salisbury Post
GIJ	Index-Journal (Greenwood, SC)	SRL	Statesville Record and Landmark
HPE	High Point Enterprise	TDS	Twin-City Daily Sentinel (Winston-Salem, NC)
HPR	The Review (High Point, NC)	WJP	Wilkes Journal-Patriot
LCJ	Louisville (KY) Courier-Journal	WP	Washington Post
LD	The Dispatch (Lexington, NC)	WS	Western Sentinel (Winston-Salem, NC)
LR	The Robesonian (Lumberton, NC)	WSJ	Winston-Salem Journal
MAN	Mount Airy News		
NT	The Tennessean (Nashville, TN)		
NWH	North Wilkesboro Hustler		

CHAPTER 1

1. *WJP*, October 10, 1985.

2. Ina W. Van Noppen and John J. Van Noppen, *Western North Carolina since the Civil War* (Boone, NC: Appalachian Consortium Press, 1973), 283.

3. NC State Board of Agriculture, *North Carolina and Its Resources* (Winston, NC: M. I. and J. C. Stewart, Public Printers and Binders, 1896), 410.

4. Sydney Nathans, *The Quest for Progress: The Way We Lived in North Carolina, 1870–1920* (Chapel Hill: University of North Carolina Press, 1983), 12–13; Johnson J. Hayes, *The Land of Wilkes* (Charlotte, NC: Heritage Printers for the Wilkes County Historical Society, 1962), 269–70.

5. Dwight B. Billings Jr., *Planters and the Making of a "New South": Class, Politics, and Development in North Carolina, 1865–1900* (Chapel Hill: University of North Carolina Press, 1979), 149.

6. "U.S. Census 1900," Historical Census Browser, www.lib.virginia.edu, accessed March 2012.

7. John Crouch, *Sketches of Wilkes* (Wilkesboro, NC: Crouch, 1902), 6.

8. Ibid., 17.

9. Yates Publishing, US and International Marriage Records, 1590–1900 (online database), Ancestry.com, accessed December 2013.

10. State of North Carolina, *An Index to Marriage Bonds Filed in the North Carolina State Archives* (Raleigh: NC Division of Archives and History, 1977).

11. War of 1812 Pension Applications, microfilm publication M313, Records of the Department of Veterans Affairs, Record Group 15, National Archives and Records Administration (hereafter NARA), Washington, DC.

12. George F. McNeil and Joyce D. McNeil, *Wilkes County Marriages Book 1—1874–1901* (Wilkesboro, NC : G. F. McNeil and J. D. McNeil, 1996). Thomas Wood is listed as nineteen years of age in 1882. US census, 1870 (online database), Ancestry.com, Rock Creek, Wilkes, North Carolina, roll M593_1165, p. 373A, image 749, Family History Library film 552664. Thomas Wood is listed as age nine, birthdate around 1861.

13. McNeil and McNeil, *Wilkes County Marriages Book 1—1874–1901.*

14. "Registration Card: Otto Harrison Wood," World War I Registration Draft Cards, 1917–1918, Ancestry.com, accessed June 2019. Various sources list Wood's birth as taking place in May 1892 or in May 1894. May 9, 1893, is the most consistent birthdate listed for Wood by his family and on official documents such as the draft registration card cited here. Hayes, *The Land of Wilkes*, 339; NC Board of Agriculture, *North Carolina and Its Resources*, 411.

15. US census, 1900 (online database), Ancestry.com, accessed September 2011; *The Record* (North Wilkesboro, NC), December 22, 2004, accessed September 19, 2011. http://www.therecordofwilkes.com/newsa.asp?edition_number=267&pg=F.

16. NC Board of Charities and Public Welfare, *Capital Punishment in North Carolina* (Raleigh: NC Board of Charities and Public Welfare, 1929), 82.

17. *NWH*, August 8, 1902.

18. Hayes, *The Land of Wilkes*, 191.

19. Wilkes County Retired School Personnel, *Lest We Forget: Education in Wilkes, 1778–1978* (Wilkesboro, NC: Wilkes County Retired School Personnel, ca. 1979), 381.

20. North Carolina, *Capital Punishment*, 82.

21. US census, 1900. Ancestry.com, accessed September 2011.

22. North Carolina, *Capital Punishment*, 82.

23. Otto Wood, *Life History of Otto Wood, Inmate, State Prison, 1926* (Raleigh: Commercial, 1926), 3–4.

24. *CO*, September 29, 1916.

25. *SRL*, January 5, 1931.

26. Ibid.

27. *CO*, September 29, 1916.

28. *SRL*, January 5, 1931.

29. Otto Wood told by Ruth Wood Holbrook to Joan Baity, archives of the Wilkes Heritage Museum, Wilkesboro, NC.

30. *Raleigh Enterprise*, December 15, 1904 (article reprinted from *Wilkesboro Chronicle*).

31. Wood, *Life History*, 5.

32. *NWH*, March 10, 1905; *NWH*, March 24, 1905.

33. *NWH*, April 12, 1907.

34. *SRL*, August 27, 1907.

35. Wood, *Life History*, 5.

36. Ibid.

37. *CO*, August 27, 1907.

38. *SRL*, September 6, 1907.

39. *SRL*, September 10, 1907.

40. *SRL*, October 11, 1907.

41. *SRL*, October 18, 1907.

42. *NWH*, April 10, 1908.

43. *LD*, September 4, 1907.

44. *CO*, February 22, 1909; *RNO*, February 21, 1909.

45. *WS*, April 13, 1909.

46. *CO*, February 22, 1909.

47. Annette Louise Bickford, *Southern Mercy: Empire and American Civilization in Juvenile Reform* (Toronto: University of Toronto Press, 2016), 169–70.

48. *Union Republican* (Winston-Salem, NC), February 25, 1909.

49. Van Noppen and Van Noppen, *Western North Carolina*, 253.

50. Wood, *Life History*, 5.

51. US census, 1900. Ancestry.com, accessed September 2011.

52. Paul H. Rakes and Kenneth Bailey, "A Hard-Bitten Lot: Nonstrike Violence in the Early Southern West Virginia Smokeless Coalfields, 1880–1910," in *Blood in the Hills: A History of Violence in Appalachia*, ed. Bruce Stewart (Lexington: University Press of Kentucky, 2012), 314–31.

53. Ibid., 473.

54. Wood, *Life History*, 5.

55. John Ed Pearce, *Days of Darkness: The Feuds of Eastern Kentucky* (Lexington: University Press of Kentucky), 74.

56. *New York Times*, March 30, 1902; *Atlanta Constitution*, March 30, 1902, and August 25, 1901; *WP*, October 24, 1911.

57. *WP*, September 20, 1906.

58. Ibid.

59. Ibid.

60. Wood, *Life History*, 5–6.

61. Ibid.; US census, 1910. Ancestry.com, accessed September 2011.

62. Wood, *Life History*, 6.

63. *Wilkes Record*, July 28, 1964.

64. Ibid.

65. Ibid.

66. Ibid.

67. *ACT*, January 3, 1931.

68. Wood, *Life History*, 5–6.

69. Ibid., 5–6.

70. Ibid., 16.

CHAPTER 2

1. *The Republican* (Clinton, MO), March 6, 1913; *Henry County Democrat* (Clinton, MO), April 17, 1913.

2. *CVN*, March 28, 1913; *Henry County Democrat* (Clinton, MO), April 17, 1913.

3. *RTD*, April 25, 1913.

4. *RTD*, April 25, 1913; "Car Robber Will Work the Roads," *CVN*, April 25, 1913.

5. Otto Wood, *Life History of Otto Wood, Inmate, State Prison, 1926* (Raleigh: Commercial, 1926), 7.

6. "Register 10: Register of Escaped," Records of the Virginia Penitentiary, series 2: Prisoner Records, 1865–1990, accession 41558, State Records Collection, Library of Virginia, Richmond.

7. Ibid.; *RTD*, May 16, 1913; *RTD*, June 29, 1913.

8. *NWH*, July 29, 1913.

9. *NWH*, August 8, 1913.

10. *NWH*, August 12, 1913.

11. Ibid.

12. *SRL*, November 25, 1926.

13. "Register 10," Records of the Virginia Penitentiary, Library of Virginia.

14. US census, 1920, Huntington Ward 4, Cabell, West Virginia, roll T625_1951, p. 1A, enumeration district 27.

15. "Register 10," Records of the Virginia Penitentiary, Library of Virginia.

16. Wood, *Life History*, 8–9.

17. *SRL*, May 12, 1924.

18. "Curbing Car Crimes: How a 100-Year-Old Car Theft Law Led to the Modern FBI," FBI.gov, October 31, 2019, https://www.fbi.gov/news/stories/how-100-year-old -car-theft-law-led-to-modern-fbi-103119.

19. *CO*, November 15, 1915; *SEP*, November 15, 1915; *GDN*, November 17, 1915.

20. *GDN*, November 17, 1915; *GDN*, November 17, 1915; *CO*, November 17, 1915.

21. *SEP*, November 19, 1915; *GDN*, November 20, 1915.

22. *SEP*, November 19, 1915.

23. *SEP*, February 5, 1916; *CO*, February 5, 1916.

24. *CO*, February 5, 1916.

25. *Statesville (NC) Sentinel*, February 10, 1916.

26. *SRL*, November 12, 1923.

27. *TDS*, September 27, 1916. For Oliver's full name, see US census, 1920, Ancestry. com, accessed November 2019. Winston-Salem Ward 1, Forsyth, NC, roll T625_1298, p. 15B, enumeration district 85. For Leak's full name, see US census, 1930, Winston-Salem, Forsyth, NC, p. 11A, enumeration district 0026, Family History Library microfilm 2341423. Ancestry.com, accessed November 2019.

28. *TDS*, September 27, 1916. *TDS*, September 28, 1916.

29. *CO*, September 27, 1916; *GDN*, September 27, 1916.

30. *SRL*, November 25, 1926.

31. *HPR*, September 28, 1916; *TDS*, September 27, 1916.

32. *TDS*, September 27, 1916. *TDS*, September 28, 1916; *NWH*, August 14, 1914; *NWH*, March 19, 1915.

33. *HPE*, September 28, 1916.

34. Ibid.

35. Ibid.; *HPE*, September 28, 1916.

36. *HPE*, September 28, 1916.

37. Kevin Young, "The World of Broadus Miller: Homicide, Lynching, and Outlawry in Early Twentieth Century North and South Carolina" (PhD diss., University of Georgia, 2016), 226–63.

38. *CO*, September 29, 1916.

39. Ibid.

40. *GDN*, September 29, 1916.

41. *HPE*, October 10, 1916; *Greensboro (NC) Patriot*, October 12, 1916.

42. *HPR*, October 12, 1916.

43. *HPR*, October 19, 1916.

44. *WS*, October 24, 1916; *GDN*, October 20, 1916; *LD*, October 25, 1916.

45. *WS*, October 24, 1916; *GDN*, October 20, 1916.

46. *HPR*, November 2, 1916; *HPE*, October 21, 1916.

47. *TDS*, October 23, 1916; *HPR*, October 26, 1916.

48. Convict Records, Tennessee State Prison Records, 1831–1992, Tennessee State Library and Archives, Nashville.

49. *CO*, June 3, 1917; *TDS*, July 9, 1917.

50. *Wilmington (NC) Morning Star*, June 4, 1917.

51. *CO*, June 3, 1917.

52. "Registration Card: Otto Harrison Wood," World War I Registration Draft Cards, 1917–1918, accessed on Ancestry.com, June 2019.

53. *NWH*, July 17, 1917.

54. *TDS*, July 9, 1917.

55. Ibid. Sewel Webster was one of the men deputized by Sheriff Woodruff to arrest Wood.

56. *Davie Record* (Mocksville, NC), July 11, 1917.

57. Luke Lea, "The Attempt to Capture the Kaiser," *Tennessee Historical Quarterly* 20, no. 3 (September 1961): 222–61.

CHAPTER 3

1. *SRL*, March 14, 1921.

2. *NT*, April 30, 1918.

3. *NT*, April 28, 1918; *Knoxville Independent*, May 4, 1918.

4. Otto Wood, *Life History of Otto Wood, Inmate, State Prison, 1926* (Raleigh: Commercial, 1926), 10–11.

5. *NT*, April 30, 1918.

6. Ibid.

7. Wood, *Life History*, 11–12.

8. Ibid.

9. *NWH*, May 3, 1918.

10. *NWH*, January 8, 1918.

11. McNeil and McNeil, *Wilkes County Marriages*, 115.

12. *Fairmont West Virginian*, January 9, 1919.

13. *HPR*, November 2, 1916.

14. Wood, *Life History*, 12.

15. See "Register 10: Register of Escaped," Records of the Virginia Penitentiary, series 2: Prisoner Records, 1865–1990, accession 41558, State Records Collection, Library of Virginia, Richmond.

16. *WSJ*, January 17, 1919.

17. US Selective Service System, World War I Selective Service System Draft

Registration Cards, 1917–1918, M1509, NARA, Washington, DC, imaged from Family History Library microfilm, registration state West Virginia, registration county Miscellaneous, roll 2022637; *Pittsburgh (PA) Press*, January 9, 1919.

18. Wood, *Life History*, 12.

19. Ibid.; *Fairmont West Virginian*, January 9, 1919.

20. Wood, *Life History*, 12.

21. *Connellsville (PA) Daily Courier*, January 9, 1919; *New Castle (PA) Herald*, January 9, 1919.

22. *Pittsburgh (PA) Press*, January 9, 1919; *Franklin (PA) News-Herald*, January 9, 1919.

23. *WSJ*, January 17, 1919.

24. Ibid.

25. *Pittsburgh (PA) Post-Gazette*, March 2, 1919.

26. NC Board of Health, Bureau of Vital Statistics, NC Death Certificates, microfilm S.123, rolls 19–242, 280, 313–682, 1040–1297, State Archives of North Carolina, Raleigh.

27. Wood, *Life History*, 13.

28. NC Board of Health, NC Death Certificates, State Archives of North Carolina.

29. *NWH*, January 31, 1919.

30. For more information on the Prohibition period in western North Carolina, see Bruce E. Stewart, *Moonshiners and Prohibitionists: The Battle over Alcohol in Southern Appalachia* (Lexington: University Press of Kentucky, 2011), 189–219.

31. Charles D. Thompson Jr., *Spirits of Just Men: Mountaineers, Liquor Bosses, and Lawmen in the Moonshine Capital of the World* (Urbana: University of Illinois Press, 2011), 150–51.

32. *NT*, February 25, 1919.

33. Ibid.

34. *NWH*, February 11, 1919.

35. Ibid.

36. For examples, see *NWH*, March 21, 1919; *NWH*, March 25, 1919; *NWH*, April 8, 1919; *NWH*, June 3, 1919.

37. *NWH*, March 21, 1919.

38. Wood, *Life History*, 13.

39. Ibid.

40. *SRL*, November 25, 1926. This interview of Rushey Hayes and G. M. Austin, Rushey's second husband confirms two children as those of Rushey and Otto Wood, living with Otto's older brother James Wood in Winston-Salem. James Wood married Rushey's sister, Esker, and the two raised the children as their own after Wood's incarceration and Rushey's marriage to G. M. Austin. The 1930 census and death certificate confirm Otto and Rushey's first child was born in January 1919.

41. *NWH*, May 16, 1919.

42. Ibid.

43. *NWH*, May 20, 1919; *WSJ*, May 20, 1919.

44. *NWH*, May 20, 1919.

45. *NWH*, May 23, 1919.

46. Wood, *Life History*, 13–14.

47. *Charleston (WV) Daily Mail*, July 3, 1919; *Shepherdstown (WV) Register*, April 24, 1919.

48. *Charleston (WV) Daily Mail*, July 3, 1919.

49. Convict Records, Tennessee State Prison Records, 1831–1992, Tennessee State Library and Archives, Nashville.

50. Ibid.

51. Ibid.

52. Wood, *Life History*, 14–15. Rushey Wood's name appears in the Winston-Salem City Directory during this period. See *Winston Salem City Directory*, Commercial Service Company, 1921. Also, a child, listed as being born January 1, 1919, appears on the 1930 census under the care of James A. Wood's household. The retrospective on Wood featured in the *Statesville Landmark* on November 25, 1926, connects these two children, born 1919 and 1923, with Otto Wood. Additional comments by family members and census records confirm these children as those of Otto Wood and Rushey Hayes. Realizing this history may be uncomfortable to some ancestors, the author has decided to leave out the complex family history left by Otto Wood in favor of charting his movements as a criminal, only connecting family members and children when necessary.

53. *SRL*, March 14, 1921.

54. Ibid.

55. Ibid.

56. *SRL*, March 23, 1921.

57. Ibid.

58. *NWH*, November 21, 1923.

59. *Houston Post*, September 5, 1921.

60. *Austin (TX) American-Statesman*, September 4, 1921.

61. Ibid.

62. Ibid.; *Houston Post*, September 5, 1921.

63. Wood, *Life History*, 20–21.

64. *PDT*, September 26, 1921.

65. Ibid.

66. *PDT*, September 28, 1921.

67. *PDT*, November 11, 1921.

68. Wood, *Life History*, 22.

69. Ohio Penitentiary Record of Escapes, November 1834–January 1928, series 1363, Archives and Library, Ohio History Connection, Columbus.

70. *LCJ*, September 16, 1923; *OMI*, September 16, 1923.

71. *LCJ*, September 16, 1923.

72. According to the US census for 1930, Rushey Hayes (Wood) had a child in 1923. Although later claimed as one of Otto Wood's, this might not be entirely possible considering Wood's release from the Ohio State Penitentiary, after serving a term of two years, in June 1923.

73. *LCJ*, September 16, 1923; *OMI*, September 16, 1923.

74. *OMI*, September 16, 1923.

75. *LCJ*, September 16, 1923.

76. *OMI*, September 13, 1923; *OMI*, September 16, 1923.

CHAPTER 4

1. *SRL*, November 19, 1923.

2. See US census, 1920 (online database). Ancestry.com, accessed November 2019.

3. *WP*, December 24, 1923.

4. *MAN*, December 10, 1925.

5. *SRL*, November 8, 1923.

6. Otto Wood, *Life History of Otto Wood, Inmate, State Prison, 1926* (Raleigh: Commercial, 1926), 13.

7. *WP*, December 24, 1923.

8. *SRL*, November 15, 1923.

9. *LCJ*, September 16, 1923; *OMI*, September 16, 1923.

10. *SRL*, November 19, 1923.

11. *SRL*, November 8, 1923.

12. *NWH*, November 14, 1923.

13. *SRL*, November 8, 1923.

14. *NWH*, November 14, 1923.

15. *OMI*, November 12, 1923; *Paducah (KY) News-Democrat*, November 13, 1923.

16. *NWH*, November 21, 1923.

17. *SRL*, November 8, 1923.

18. Ibid.; *SRL*, November 19, 1923.

19. *SRL*, November 8, 1923.

20. *SRL*, November 15, 1923.

21. *SRL*, November 19, 1923.

22. Ibid.

23. Ibid.

24. *NWH*, November 21, 1923.

25. *SRL*, November 19, 1923.

26. *SRL*, December 24, 1923; *MAN*, December 27, 1923.

27. *MAN*, December 27, 1923.

28. Ibid.

29. Ibid.

30. *WJP*, January 3, 1924.

31. Ibid.

32. *Greensburg Tribune* (Pittsburgh, PA), January 12, 1931.

33. *WP*, May 11, 1924; *WP*, May 12, 1924; *L D* , May 12, 1924.

34. *WJP*, May 15, 1924.

35. *NWH*, May 14, 1924; *SRL*, May 12, 1924.

36. *SRL*, May 12, 1924.

37. Ibid.

38. Ibid.

39. Ibid.

40. *DB*, May 13, 1924.

41. Ibid.

42. *SRL*, May 15, 1924.

43. *DB*, May 15, 1924.

44. *SRL*, May 15, 1924.

45. *SRL*, May 19, 1924.

46. *DB*, May 15, 1924.

47. *SRL*, May 15, 1924. Additionally, the *Winston-Salem City Directory* (1921) confirms Rushey Wood as a resident of the city. Esker Hayes, Rushey's sister and wife of James A. Wood, also lived in Winston-Salem making it possible that this was the household discussed in Rushey Wood's interview with Chief of Police Taylor.

48. *SRL*, May 15, 1924.

49. *SRL*, November 25, 1926.

50. *Hartford (CT) Courant*, June 16, 1924.

51. Ibid.

52. *LD*, May 12, 1924.

53. *SRL*, May 12, 1924.

54. *SRL*, May 15, 1924.

55. Ibid.

56. *SRL*, June 5, 1924.

57. *WJP*, August 28, 1924.

58. *SRL*, August 21, 1924.

59. *SRL*, May 29, 1924.

60. *SRL*, June 5, 1924.

61. Ibid.

CHAPTER 5

1. *MAN*, December 10, 1925.

2. Ibid.

3. *NWH*, December 2, 1925.

4. Ibid.

5. *GDG*, November 25, 1925.

6. Ibid.

7. *MAN*, December 10, 1925.

8. *DB*, December 2, 1925.

9. *NWH*, December 9, 1925.

10. *MAN*, December 10, 1925.

11. *Albemarle (NC) Press*, December 10, 1925.

12. *MAN*, December 10, 1925.

13. Ibid. The antisemitic comment was reportedly made to Guilford County deputy sheriff John A. Hobbs. Hobbs reported seeing Wood in Raleigh while dropping prisoners a week before Wood's escape. Wood's target, per Hobbs, was Charles Hyman who testified against Wood at the 1924 trial for the murder of Kaplan in Greensboro. See *NWH*, December 2, 1925. Wood's threats against M. G. Austin of Winston-Salem, NC, are detailed in *MAN*, December 3, 1925.

14. *GDG*, July 10, 1926.

15. Ibid.

16. Ibid.

17. *MAN*, July 15, 1926.

18. *MAN*, September 9, 1926.

19. *WJP*, July 15, 1926.

20. *GDG*, July 10, 1926.

21. Ibid.

22. *WJP*, July 15, 1926.

23. *GDG*, July 10, 1926.

24. Ibid.

25. Ibid.

26. *SRL*, August 9, 1926.

27. *DB*, November 23, 1926; *GDG*, November 22, 1926.

28. Ibid.

29. Ibid.

30. *SRL*, November 23, 1926.

31. Ibid.

32. *DB*, November 23, 1926; *GDG*, November 23, 1926.

33. *SRL*, November 22, 1926.

34. *DB*, November 23, 1926.

35. *SRL*, November 22, 1926.

36. *DB*, November 23, 1926.

37. *SRL*, November 25, 1926.

38. *DB*, November 23, 1926.

39. *SRL*, November 25, 1926.

40. Ibid.

41. Ibid.

42. *SRL*, December 2, 1926.

43. *SRL*, December 6, 1926.

44. *SRL*, November 25, 1926.

45. *SRL*, December 6, 1926.

46. *SRL*, December 2, 1926.

47. Ibid.

48. *DB*, November 26, 1926.

49. *SRL*, November 25, 1926.

50. Ibid.

51. *SRL*, December 6, 1926; *GDG*, December 4, 1926.

52. *SRL*, December 6, 1926.

53. *SRL*, December 6, 1926.

54. Ibid.; *GDG*, December 4, 1926.

55. *GDG*, December 4, 1926.

56. *SRL*, December 6, 1926.

57. *SRL*, January 3, 1927.

58. *DB*, January 12, 1927.

59. *SRL*, January 17, 1927.

60. *Muncie (IN) Evening Press*, January 26, 1927.

61. *SRL*, January 14, 1927.

62. *GDG*, February 2, 1927; *Indianapolis News*, February 18, 1927; Otto Wood, *Life History of Otto Wood, Inmate, State Prison, 1926*, 1931 postscript (1926; Raleigh: Commercial, 1931), 36. Prison officials, in writing a postscript to Wood's autobiography, remembered that he enjoyed showing off the change purse that deflected the bullet away from his heart.

63. *GDG*, February 14, 1927.
64. Ibid.
65. *SRL*, February 17, 1927.
66. *SRL*, February 21, 1927.
67. *DB*, February 22, 1927.
68. *GDG*, February 22, 1927.
69. *SRL*, February 28, 1927.
70. *SRL*, May 2, 1927.
71. Ibid.
72. *SRL*, March 24, 1927.
73. *GDG*, April 2, 1927.
74. *Daily Tar Heel* (Chapel Hill, NC), May 26, 1927.
75. *GDG*, July 4, 1927.
76. *SRL*, October 21, 1927.
77. *DB*, May 22, 1928; *RNO*, May 10, 1928.

CHAPTER 6

1. *Spartanburg (SC) Herald-Journal*, July 15, 1930.
2. Joseph L. Morrison, *Governor O. Max Gardner: A Power in North Carolina and New Deal Washington* (Chapel Hill: University of North Carolina Press, 1971), 6, 52.
3. Edwin Gill, secretary, *Public Papers and Letters of Oliver Max Gardner: Governor of North Carolina 1929–1933*, ed. David Leroy Corbitt (Raleigh: Council of State for the State of North Carolina, 1937), 32.
4. Ibid., 32–33, 490–91, 599.
5. NC State Board of Charities and Public Welfare, *Capital Punishment in North Carolina* (Raleigh: NC State Board of Charities and Public Welfare, 1929), 84–85.
6. Ibid., 80, 86.
7. Ibid., 7.
8. Otto Wood, *Life History of Otto Wood, Inmate, State Prison, 1926*, 1931 postscript (1926; Raleigh: Commercial, 1931), 36; *ACT*, September 7, 1930.
9. *SRL*, July 22, 1929.
10. Ibid.
11. Ibid.
12. *DB*, August 21, 1929.
13. Morrison, *Governor O. Max Gardner*, 54, 61, 75.
14. *MAN*, May 22, 1930.
15. *Sarasota (FL) Herald*, January 6, 1930.
16. *Florence (AL) Times Daily*, January 14, 1930.
17. *MAN*, October 31, 1929.
18. *MAN*, May 22, 1930.
19. *WJP*, May 22, 1930.
20. *ACT*, September 7, 1930.
21. *Los Angeles Times*, July 12, 1930.
22. *SRL*, May 22, 1930.
23. Wood, *Life History* (1931), 37.

24. *San Jose Evening News*, July 11, 1930.

25. *AS*, July 12, 1930.

26. Wood, *Life History* (1931), 38.

27. *AS*, July 14, 1930.

28. Wood, *Life History* (1931), 38.

29. *BDT*, September 22, 1930.

30. *Hartford (CT) Courant*, July 21, 1930.

31. *SRL*, July 17, 1930.

32. Ibid.

33. *SRL*, September 22, 1930.

34. *SRL*, July 14, 1930.

35. *Spartanburg (SC) Herald-Journal*, July 15, 1930.

36. *SRL*, August 25, 1930.

37. *AS*, July 14, 1930.

38. *SRL*, September 8, 1930.

39. *WJP*, September 25, 1930.

40. Ibid.; *ACT*, December 23, 1928.

41. *SRL*, September 25, 1930; *SRL*, November 17, 1931.

42. *SRL*, September 22, 1930.

43. *BDT*, September 22, 1930.

44. *SRL*, September 22, 1930.

45. Ibid.

46. *ACT*, September 21, 1930.

47. *SRL*, September 25, 1930.

48. *LR*, September 18, 1930.

49. *WJP*, October 16, 1930.

50. *MAN*, October 9, 1930.

51. *WJP*, October 9, 1930.

52. *SRL*, September 22, 1930.

53. *BDT*, November 7, 1930.

CHAPTER 7

1. *SP*, January 19, 1931.

2. *SP*, January 3, 1931.

3. Ibid.; *SP*, January 1, 1931; *MAN*, January 1, 1931. According to sources used to investigate the whereabouts of Roy Banner Barker, Wood told people in Wilkes County about spending time in tourist parks near Bristol before returning to Virginia and then to North Carolina.

4. *SP*, January 19, 1931. Barker only ever reported one occupation in census records, "Helper" in his family's restaurant at the age of fourteen. See US censuses for 1920, 1930, and 1940, Ancestry.com, accessed November 2019.. His death certificate records heart failure as the cause of death. See Virginia, Death Records, 1912–2014. Whether Barker was perhaps physically unable to work or mentally impaired is unclear in the records. No evidence is forthcoming that he had any run-ins in with the law, besides those in the company of Wood, casting some doubt on the fact that his not reporting any vocation was due to criminal activities. William Somers, sheriff of Wilkes County, later acknowledged Barker had been in the

county weeks earlier and stated that he could not connect Barker to any crimes. For bootlegging charges, see *SP*, January 1, 1931.

5. *SP*, January 19, 1931. The details on dialogue come from a report rendered to Rowan County judge Clyde E. Gooch after investigation into Wood's movements in Wilkes County, reprinted in the *Salisbury Post* after the exoneration of Roy Banner Barker. Silas Johnson's name was misprinted as "Johnston" in the report. See *Find a Grave Index*, 1600s–Current, Silas Washington Johnson, Antioch Baptist Church Cemetery (buried), Wilkesboro, Wilkes County, NC. The report also mangled the name of Eva Shew with the interviewers recording the name of Eva Shew phonetically as "Shoe." One of Silas Johnson's children, Magalene Johnson Bynum, later corroborated much of the story told by Johnson in a 1991 interview with the *Winston-Salem Journal*. See *WSJ*, December 8, 1991.

6. *SP*, January 19, 1931.

7. Ibid.

8. Ibid.

9. Ibid.

10. *SP*, January 1, 1931.

11. Ibid.

12. *LR*, January 1, 1931; Otto Wood, *Life History of Otto Wood, Inmate, State Prison, 1926*, 1931 postscript (1926; repr., Raleigh: Commercial, 1931), 40. The report of Chief Rankin featured in *Life History* places the time for when authorities were tipped off about Wood's presence closer to 1 p.m. For full names of Rankin and Kessler see US census, 1920.

13. *ACT*, January 9, 1931.

14. *SRL*, January 5, 1931.

15. *LR*, January 1, 1931; *RHH*, December 31, 1930.

16. *LR*, January 1, 1931; Wood, *Life History* (1931), 40. The 1931 postscript of Wood's *Life History*, written by prison officials, describes Wood cursing in his response to Rankin asking to see his hand.

17. *BDT*, December 31, 1930; Wood, *Life History* (1931), 40–41. The 1931 postscript of Wood's *Life History*, written by prison officials, describes the caliber of Wood's pistol.

18. *LR*, January 1, 1931.

19. Wood, *Life History* (1931), 40–41.

20. *SRL*, January 5, 1931.

21. Wood, *Life History* (1931), 40–41.

22. *GIJ*, January 1, 1931; *SRL*, January 1, 1931; Wood, *Life History* (1931), 40–41.

23. *SRL*, January 1, 1931.

24. Wood, *Life History* (1931), 40–41; *Rocky Mount (NC) Telegram*, March 11, 1979.

25. Wood, *Life History* (1931), 40–41.

26. *GIJ*, January 1, 1931.

27. *SRL*, January 1, 1931.

28. *GIJ*, January 1, 1931.

29. Wood, *Life History* (1931), 40–41.

30. *SRL*, January 1, 1931.

31. Wood, *Life History* (1931), 40–41. This account is nearly identical to one printed in *LR*, January 1, 1931.

32. *SRL*, January 1, 1931.

33. *RHH*, December 31, 1930.

34. NC Board of Health, Bureau of Vital Statistics, NC Death Certificates, micro-film S.123, rolls 19–242, 280, 313–682, 1040–1297, State Archives of North Carolina, Raleigh.

35. *GIJ*, January 1, 1931.

36. *SP*, January 3, 1931.

37. *SP*, January 19, 1931.

38. *SRL*, January 22, 1931.

39. *BDT*, February 25, 1931.

40. *SRL*, January 5, 1931.

41. *BDT*, January 2, 1931.

42. "General Index to Vital Statistics—Guilford County, N.C.—Births," North Carolina, Birth Indexes 1800–2000. Celia Byrd is listed as having two children on March 25, 1931, "Ruby Olivia Wood" and "Rueben G. Wood."

43. *SP*, January 1, 1931.

44. *LR*, January 1, 1931; *SP*, January 1, 1931.

45. *SP*, January 1, 1931.

46. *SP*, January 3, 1931.

47. Ibid.

48. *SRL*, January 5, 1931.

49. Ibid.

50. *SRL*, January 5, 1931.

51. *SP*, January 5, 1931.

52. *SRL*, January 5, 1931.

53. *SP*, January 5, 1931.

54. *SRL*, January 5, 1931.

55. *Greenville (SC) News*, January 5, 1931.

56. *Honolulu Advertiser*, January 31, 1931; *Green Bay Press-Gazette*, January 29, 1931.

57. *WJP*, January 1, 1931.

58. *MAN*, January 1, 1931.

59. Ibid.

60. *SRL*, January 5, 1931.

61. Ibid.

62. Ibid.

63. Ibid.

64. *MAN*, January 1, 1931.

65. *WJP*, February 12, 1931.

66. Joseph L. Morrison, *Governor O. Max Gardner: A Power in North Carolina and New Deal Washington* (Chapel Hill: University of North Carolina Press, 1971), 94–95.

CHAPTER 8

1. Kip Lornell, *Virginia's Blues, Country, and Gospel Records: 1902–1943: An Annotated Bibliography* (Lexington: University Press of Kentucky, 1989), 170.

2. Ibid.

3. *BDT*, March 20, 1931.

4. Ibid.

5. *BDT*, November 11, 1932.

6. *LD*, May 22, 1933.

7. *SRL*, January 8, 1931 (reprinted from *Greensboro News*).

8. *LR*, January 15, 1931.

9. Tony Russell and Bob Pinson, *Country Music Records: A Discography, 1921–1942* (New York: Oxford University Press, 2004), 731.

10. "Otto Wood," *In the Pines: Tar Heel Folk Songs and Fiddle Tunes* (Raleigh: Old Hat Records, 2008).

11. Kinney Rorrer, "Off the Record: Otto Wood the Bandit," *Old Time Herald* 9, no. 6 (Winter 2004–5): 18.

12. "Otto Wood," by Cranford and Thompson, Champion 17486, recorded January 27, 1931, Richmond, IN.

13. Rorrer, "Off the Record," 19.

14. Patrick Sky, "'Otto Wood the Bandit': A North Carolina Ballad," *North Carolina Folklore Journal* 41, no. 1 (Winter–Spring 1994): 43.

15. Rorrer, "Off the Record," 19.

16. *WJP*, March 12, 1931.

17. Ibid.

18. "Otto Wood the Bandit," by the Carolina Buddies, Columbia 151345-2, recorded February 24, 1931, New York, NY.

19. Norm Cohen, "Walter 'Kid' Smith," *JEMF Quarterly* 9, no. 3 (Autumn 1973): 130.

20. Tony Russell, *Country Music: The Legends and the Lost* (New York: Oxford University Press, 2010), 143–44.

21. Rorrer, "Off the Record," 19.

22. Russell and Pinson, *Country Music Records*, 842.

23. *DB*, March 27, 1931.

24. "Otto Wood, the Bandit," by Slim Smith, Victor Records 67436-1, February 5, 1931, New York, NY.

25. *MAN*, January 1, 1931.

26. *Rockingham (NC) Post-Dispatch*, April 28, 1932.

27. Otto Wood, *Life History of Otto Wood, Inmate, State Prison, 1926* (Raleigh: Commercial, 1926), 7.

28. Rorrer, "Off the Record," 19.

29. Matthew J. C. Hodgart, *The Ballads* (New York: W. W. Norton and Company, 1962), 17.

30. Sky, "'Otto Wood the Bandit,'" 40.

31. Ibid., 43.

32. Doc Watson and Merle Watson, *Doc Watson and Son* (LP, Vanguard, 1965).

33. The Possum Hunters, *Death on the Highway (and Other Southern Lullabies)* (LP, Takoma, 1966).

34. *Old Time Ballads from the Southern Appalachian Mountains: Recorded 1927–1931* (LP, County 522, 1972).

35. '68 Comeback, *Mr. Downchild* (LP, Sympathy for the Record Industry—SFTRI 277, 1994).

36. Snatches of Pink, *Hyena* (CD, MoRisen Records—MR-7770, 2003).

37. Larry Shores, *Songs of T-Town* (CD, Pinnacle Productions—Music Maker Relief Foundation, 2006).

38. *NWR*, November 24, 2004.

39. *NWR*, December 8, 2004.

40. Elkville String Band, *Over the Mountain* (CD, Mountain Roads Recordings, 2008).

41. *NWR*, June 22, 2011.

42. *SP*, June 11, 2014. This production won multiple awards from the North Carolina Society of Historians, including an award for Otto Wood himself. The bandit was posthumously awarded the Robert Bruce Cooke Family History Book Award.

CONCLUSION

1. See Eric Hobsbawm, *Bandits* (London: Orion, 2010).

SUGGESTED READINGS
ON APPALACHIAN CRIME AND MUSIC

Fussell, Fred C., with Steve Kruger. *Blue Ridge Music Trails of North Carolina: A Guide to Sites, Artists, and Traditions of the Mountains and Foothills*. Chapel Hill: University of North Carolina Press, 2018.

Huber, Patrick. *Linthead Stomp: The Creation of Country Music in the Piedmont South*. Chapel Hill: University of North Carolina Press, 2008.

Pierce, Daniel S. *Corn from a Jar: Moonshining in the Great Smoky Mountains*. Gatlinburg, TN: Great Smoky Mountains Association, 2013.

———. *Tar Heel Lightning: How Secret Stills and Fast Cars Made North Carolina the Moonshine Capital of the World*. Chapel Hill: University of North Carolina Press, 2019.

Stewart, Bruce E., ed. *Blood in the Hills: A History of Violence in Appalachia*. Lexington: University Press of Kentucky, 2018.

———. *Moonshiners and Prohibitionists: The Battle over Alcohol in Southern Appalachia*. Lexington: University Press of Kentucky, 2011.

Thompson, Charles D., Jr. *Spirits of Just Men: Mountaineers, Liquor Bosses, and Lawmen in the Moonshine Capital of the World*. Champaign-Urbana: University of Illinois Press, 2011.

Williams, John A. *Appalachia: A History*. Chapel Hill: University of North Carolina Press, 2002.

INDEX